Schools for the
21st Century

SCHOOL LEADERSHIP AND MANAGEMENT SERIES

Series Editors: Brent Davies and John West-Burnham

Other titles in the series:

Effective Learning in Schools
by Christopher Bowring-Carr and John West-Burnham

Effective School Leaders
by John MacBeath and Kate Myers

From Bursar to School Business Manager
Reengineering leadership for resource management
by Fergus O'Sullivan, Angela Thody and Elizabeth Wood

Leadership and Professional Development in Schools
How to promote techniques for effective professional learning
by John West-Burnham and Fergus O'Sullivan

Managing Learning for Achievement
Strategies for raising achievement through effective learning
edited by Christopher Bowring-Carr and John West-Burnham

Managing Quality in Schools (2nd edition)
by John West-Burnham

Middle Management in Schools
How to harmonise managing and teaching for an effective school
by Sonia Blandford

Reengineering and Total Quality in Schools
edited by Brent Davies and John West-Burnham

Resource Management in Schools
Effective and practical strategies for the self-managing school
by Sonia Blandford

Strategic Marketing for Schools
How to integrate marketing and strategic development for an effective school
by Brent Davies and Linda Ellison

Heads in Partnership
by Joan Sallis

Forthcoming titles:

Performance Management in Schools
edited by John West-Burnham, John O'Neill and Ingrid Bradbury

Working with Support Staff
by Trevor Kerry

Schools for the 21st Century

Developing best practice

IRENE DALTON, RICHARD FAWCETT
AND JOHN WEST-BURNHAM

An imprint of **Pearson Education**

London · New York · San Francisco · Toronto · Sydney · Tokyo · Singapore
Hong Kong · Cape Town · Madrid · Paris · Milan · Munich · Amsterdam

PEARSON EDUCATION LIMITED

Head Office:
Edinburgh Gate
Harlow CM20 2JE
Tel: +44 (0)1279 623623
Fax: +44 (0)1279 431059

London Office:
128 Long Acre, London WC2E 9AN
Tel: +44 (0)20 7447 2000
Fax: +44 (0)20 7240 5771
Website: www.educationminds.com

First published in Great Britain in 2001

© Pearson Education Limited 2001
© Chapter 7 Colin Greenhalgh 2001

The right of Irene Dalton, Richard Fawcett and John West-Burnham to be
identified as authors of this work has been asserted by them in accordance
with the Copyright, Designs and Patents Act 1988.

ISBN 0 273 65441 1

British Library Cataloguing in Publication Data
A CIP catalogue record for this book can be obtained from the British Library.

10 9 8 7 6 5 4 3 2 1

Typeset by Pantek Arts Ltd., Maidstone, Kent.
Printed and bound in Great Britain.

The Publishers' policy is to use paper manufactured from sustainable forests.

About the Contributors

■   ■   ■

Geoff Barton is deputy head at Thurston Community College, Suffolk.

Keith Cox is assistant head at Hipperholme and Lightcliffe High School in Yorkshire.

Irene Dalton is head of Wombwell High School, Barnsley. She is editor of the Secondary Heads Association (SHA) house journal, *Headlines*.

Richard Fawcett is headteacher of Thurston Upper School in Suffolk. He is president of the Secondary Heads Association for 2000–2001.

Mike Foley is deputy headteacher at Thurston Community College, Suffolk.

Colin Greenhalgh, OBE, DL is principal of Hills Road Sixth Form College, Cambridge.

Kate Griffin is head of Greenford High School in the London Borough of Ealing.

Mike Hardacre is director of Wolverhampton Education Action Zone.

Tony Hinkley is deputy head at Ellowes Hall School in Dudley in the West Midlands.

Dame Tamsyn Imison, DBE, is an education strategist and was recently head-teacher of Hampstead School in North London.

Mo Laycock is head of Firth Park Community College, Sheffield.

Malcolm Noble is headteacher of Bexleyheath School in Kent.

John Read is deputy head of Wombwell High School, Barnsley.

Bernard Trafford is head of Wolverhampton Grammar School, a co-educational independent day school.

John West-Burnham is Professor of Educational Leadership at the International Leadership Centre, University of Hull.

About the Series Editors

Professor Brent Davies, PhD. Brent is Director of the International Leadership Centre at the University of Hull. Brent works exclusively on headteacher and senior staff development programmes in the UK and in Australia, New Zealand and the United States of America. He has written 11 books and published over 50 articles.

John West-Burnham. John is Professor of Educational Leadership at the International Leadership Centre, University of Hull. After 15 years as a school-teacher he has worked for five universities and as an LEA adviser. He is the author or editor of 14 books and has worked in eight countries as lecturer and consultant.

Contents

■ ■ ■

Introduction

■ ■ ■

This is a book about making the difference.

Leaders in schools, the members of the leadership team, are inventive, inspirational and, in the best of circumstances, insistent that 'how we do things here' reflects an unswerving confidence that they know what is best for their students. In short, what happens in the school is their agenda, not one imposed from outside.

Creating a vision means having the capacity and confidence to draw people into the centre of a leadership team's thinking. How priorities and development plans are defined will be a matter for discussion, debate, consultation and analysis. Staff, governors, parents and students will all have much to contribute. However, at the centre of inspiration lie the leadership team's values, creativity, passion, enthusiasm and excitement for education.

Improvement is one of today's watchwords. School improvement very often means implementing someone else's policy and in particular that of the government. While we all want to continue to raise standards of literacy and numeracy, for example, school leaders want much more than that for their students. They wish to see improvement stemming from within. They have their own ideas and agenda for change. And quite rightly so.

What lies beyond the sigmoid curve? How are schools to continue to raise standards and achievements that include, but stretch beyond, examinations and tests? Year on year, standards are rising. The curve of improvement for most schools is real. But for how long will we see continued academic progress solely through turning up the burner's flame under literacy and numeracy, and the exclusive five A*–C target? Anyhow, is that the sole ambition for our students? It is not.

Building the capacity to change, keeping everyone focused on year-on-year improvement over all areas of education, means focusing on the people in the school who make things happen – building to last. We must do more than concentrate solely and directly on tests and examinations if we are to continue the upward progress of educational achievement. The key is transformation, making the difference over broad areas of school life, and this is happening now in many of our schools.

This book is a collection of 11 examples of individual practice, the public tip of an iceberg of creativity and innovation alongside the pressure of agendas originating beyond school. The first six contributions offer a discussion of broad issues reconceptualising schools; the rest focus on specific innovations and ideas, work that has changed schools for the better of students in them.

1

■ ■ ■

School Leadership: If It's Such a Tough Job, How Do People Do It?

by Bernard Trafford

Introduction: a tough job

We create small communities where the truth matters. We do not tolerate bullies. We can, simply by walking down the school hall, still cause 500 15–16 year-olds to fall silent. We set examples of courtesy, treat students with respect, raise their self-esteem, and are counted upon to give a fair hearing. Our leadership is tested daily and we have no security guards, no speechwriters, and no spin doctors to stand between us and the public. We are not afraid to expose what we believe in because it might make us unpopular, therefore our beliefs in justice, equal value and integrity will make a difference immediately in the school and, with faith and over time, in the wider community.

(Dalton, 2000)

So writes Irene Dalton, a secondary school head, in her editorial for the November edition of the magazine which she edits for her professional association, the Secondary Heads Association. It is a strong statement about the complexity of the task of school leadership and the extent to which huge moral authority is vested in a single person. This view accords with findings published by consultants Hay McBer who compared the role of headteacher with that of many leaders in business and industry: the school job was seen as far more complex and demanding (Kelly, 2000). Indeed, the more the job is analysed, the more we may wonder whether it can be done at all. Is it actually possible to balance *so many* conflicting pressures and demands? It is certainly hard, but it *is* done, and effectively, by many very able school leaders. The evidence is there. There *are* people out there running schools successfully in an enormous range of settings. Recently I found myself at a dinner sitting next to a headhunter who, among other things, was trying to find new careers for a number of headteachers who wanted to move into different fields of work. 'The trouble is,' she told me, 'after the job that they have been doing it's very hard to find them one that is challenging enough even to keep them interested.'

So who are these 'highly effective' school leaders? Are they born or made? Do they move into that truly extraordinary role ready formed? The well-publicised experience of so-called 'superheads' suggests not. Later in this chapter I will discuss how even an experienced headteacher, 'parachuted in' to a difficult school, needs more than the wealth of experience already gained in order to grow into a new setting and turn around a difficult situation. This concept of growth is, I believe, also central to the process of someone taking over a school leadership post for the first time. In this chapter I hope to demonstrate that the job is possible, but it cannot be done solo. Leaders need to have teams and allies around them and at the heart of the challenge for school leaders is the need both to win those allies and to have the courage to delegate power to them so that the leaders can in return receive their allies' support. School leadership is all about change and improvement, and to achieve those things leaders must be able to persuade and inspire. So they need remarkable amounts of inner strength and patience.

There is no blueprint, no single way of doing it. Indeed, when school leaders try to apply pre-formed management solutions the schemes tend to end in failure. But there are, of course, always things that can be learned from the experience of others. The experiences that I describe in the next section are simply examples, some of things that went right and others of things I have got entirely wrong, but from which I hope I have learned. The tale that I recount refers to my experience of becoming a head at the age of 34; but I think that the process of growing into the role has close parallels to taking on management responsibility at any level in education.

One head's experience

Starting out

I cannot claim that I began my new headship with a complete and clear vision of the job, despite my nine years' knowledge of the same school as a middle manager. Of course I wanted it to be the 'best possible' school, providing the finest and broadest opportunities it could to its students and, perhaps less worthily, maintaining and increasing its reputation both locally and nationally. I wanted the students to feel happy and valued, and wanted to be approachable myself. I do remember feeling that we needed a clearer sense of purpose in the school, that we needed somehow to increase our students' sense of commitment to their education. And I remember, at my very first staff meeting, gaining agreement that it would be school policy always to refer to students by their first name, finally abandoning the old-fashioned boys' grammar school tradition (by then honoured far more in the breach than in the observance) of using their surnames.

With regard to my management of the teaching body, I had one clear aim. I was convinced that we needed to improve communication, develop a more closely shared sense of purpose, and ensure that everyone had a voice that could be heard so that everyone could contribute ideas to the running and improvement of the school. From the start I used the word *democratic* to describe the management style I wished to adopt. This was certainly a matter of principle for me, a deliberate attempt to change the prevailing culture within the staff in the belief that a participative approach would be both welcome and productive.

Getting everyone involved

The theory was in general welcomed, but in practice the change was fraught with difficulties. Early meetings were frequently stormy. Part of the reason for this was the release of a certain amount of frustration, of colleagues getting things off their chest. Partly it was because all of us, myself included, needed to learn the skills that would ensure that debate would be open, frank, yet courteous. The staff had long enjoyed a strong sense of collegiality, but this was in some tension with the traditional territorialism of departments. Heads of department, in particular, often felt that they had to protect the interests of their individual fiefdom. Achieving a new balance between promoting the interests of individual subject areas and those of the whole school (not forgetting that this is all for the benefit of the students!) was perhaps one of the last things to be achieved in our meetings.

Notwithstanding that reservation, when I became head I felt that I was leading a staff whose approach was, like my own, to put the interests and needs of our students at the forefront of everything that they did. I have always been proud that the school makes decisions on the basis of the students' interest, not of teacher or administrative convenience. To my surprise, I soon found that such sincerely felt yet unarticulated principles were not at all clearly perceived by the student body.

In my first term as head, I was close to completing a part-time MEd course in Education Policy and Management at Birmingham University. I had completed the core modules (organisation/management theory; economics; law; staff development and appraisal) and, by way of contrast, had opted to follow a module run by Roland Meighan, author/co-editor of *A Sociology of Educating* and *The Democratic School*. Meighan, who describes himself as an educational free-thinker, has long made it his business to encourage his students to look at schools and education from viewpoints other than the institutional and orthodox. He introduced me to Edward Blishen's fascinating book *The School That I'd Like*, a compilation of the responses received when a Sunday newspaper invited schoolchildren to write on that title. Stimulated by this, I went into my own classrooms and asked the students what they thought of the education they were receiving and how they would like to see it improved. The results were electrifying, and also worrying:

> *There were, to be sure, many examples of things that they liked and valued in a fundamentally and happy and productive school, and a number of selfish preoccupations, but I was astonished, and often shocked, by the number of things that made them insecure or unhappy. There were numerous perceived injustices – put-downs by teachers, absurd rules, unfair pressures, unkindness between students, unkindness by teachers, numerous institutional contradictions and inconsistencies which rankled and soured an otherwise happy educational experience. I soon came to believe that the students, too, must be brought into the dialogue, both because their right to respect as thinking individuals must be strengthened and because they had vital things to say about the education that the school was attempting to provide for them.*

> *(Trafford, 1997: 4–5)*

Meanwhile, staff discussions were leading us to the conclusion that we needed to encourage our students to take more responsibility for their school lives and learning. It was recognised that, if they were to do this, they would need to be given more power over their school lives. Thus from two directions came the realisation that we needed some process of empowerment of the students if we were to help them to develop the motivation and sense of responsibility that would make them more effective and successful learners. I charted developments in the school over the first five years or so as the democratic approach developed with regard to both students and teachers, writing up the research in a doctoral thesis.

There were many lessons that needed to be learned by all of us. The fact that it is nice to have our voice heard, and to have our way, has to be balanced with the need for compromise. Students needed to learn when particular types of issues should and should not be raised, particularly when these would have an impact on individuals, and we had to devise mechanisms so that such issues could be addressed in a proper and fair way. We all had to learn how to come to appropriate decisions when it was difficult to determine whose opinion should hold sway: for example, when we had differences of opinion between parents, students and staff over issues of school policy. Some of these issues, particularly in the early years, were challenging and stressful for all of us. Sometimes I felt under siege as frustrations surfaced and anger was vented. Frequently harsh criticism was directed at 'the school' or 'management': I tended to take this personally, partly because it was intended that I should, and partly because I was over-sensitive.

How getting people involved brings about school improvement

After ten years of headship I now feel able to look back, not just to see what has been achieved but also to try to find what lessons can be drawn from all that work and change. Even in 1996, when writing up the results of my research, I was able to demonstrate that the school was not simply happier, and school life richer, but that it was more effective as a result. Not only was evidence of improved academic standards provided by value-added measures (still in their infancy then), but my research was also able to link that improvement to the changed atmosphere and ethos of the school.

The progress identified in 1996 has been continued since. There is much more clarity, both in the school's day-to-day operation and in the way that decisions are made; an unexpected development, from my point of view, is that openness demands a great deal more writing than I had thought. Clarity requires that policies and procedures are written down and clear for all to understand. Consistency and fairness, instead of being by-products of a generally student-friendly and happy school, are part of the fabric and the ethos; again, they are written down as aims, and channels for those who seek justice or redress are stated and easily followed in what we call the *school philosophy and school rules*. School teachers always like to feel they are approachable, but we too often delude ourselves. My school now has mechanisms and printed policies that *require* those of us in authority to be approachable. Students are not forced to follow one particular channel if it does not suit them. Indeed, the (printed) ground rule for all students *and* teachers is that anyone can take their problems to anyone at all with whom they feel comfortable, with the assurance that they will not be fobbed off. Time after time this is proved to work not only in theory but also in practice. Mutual respect is a central aim, not a by-product, of the ethos, and is an essential ingredient of the process of discussion, negotiation and compromise.

Central to the empowerment of our students has been the Student Council which has been running for nine years. The minutes of its meetings were kept irregularly at first but meticulously for the past five or six years, and are now published throughout the school. The collected minutes are a fascinating record both of the development of democracy within the school and of the way in which the student body has constantly questioned not only how the school works but also how its own democracy operates. The Student Council is a symbol that reminds everyone that our students really do have a voice and a right to be heard; it is also an effective mechanism for bringing about change. I always attend its weekly meetings (though I did not at first – a mistake). I often say that I find it one of the most stimulating times of the week:

> *I am asked to explain why something is done – or why I can't change it. Frequently we plan together a significant improvement that will benefit everyone. I think it important that the head is not only accessible but also accountable – at these meetings, I am both. These sessions really do serve to empower the students.*

> *(Trafford, 2000)*

So we have established and promoted the concept of our students having a right to a voice in, and power over, their own education. It should be clear by now that I believe this has ensured that our students' happiness, confidence and self-esteem are at the heart of what we do in the school, not merely happy accidents within a benign regime. This is not just my impression. In the early years, when I was using questionnaires and interviews to try to measure what change, if any, was actually taking place, I received resounding endorsements of change for the better. Students who had witnessed the changes from the start gave invaluable insights about how their whole educational experience was now more positive:

> *The Student Council is as good as it will get … you'd see a noticeable change if you walked round. (Year 13 student, 1995)*

> *It was very severe before. (Year 13 student, 1995)*

> *There is less racism and bullying now. Girls are accepted now. (Year 7 and Year 9 students, 1995)*

> *Staff are happier, kids are happier. (Teacher, 1995)*

> *Liberality, less stuffy atmosphere, diversity, room for experimentation, more of a feeling of 'our school' (Teacher 1995)*

> *Most students feel they will be listened to by most members of staff. (Teacher 1995)*

> *(Trafford, 1997: 68–69)*

A new arrival in the sixth form described the change from her previous school:

> *It is a good deal more democratic than my previous school – I am not afraid to voice my opinion … From day one I have felt free to speak openly and complain if necessary.*

> *(Trafford, 1997: 11)*

Other students felt that they were more aware of each other's cultures: one student identified inter-racial friendship groups as directly attributable to democratic changes. A teacher put it thus:

> *It makes for security all round. Students can feel that if they have got a serious grudge or problem, they can say something. Also for staff … everyone feels valued, they work together and learn.*

> *(Harber and Trafford, 1999: 49)*

How it works in practice

Five years after most of those views were gathered, circumstantial evidence constantly crops up to illustrate the difference between this school and the traditional authoritarian model. Recently a visiting inspector was asking how the management in practice related to the printed version of the structure. 'Who drives change?' he asked. 'Who pushes the levers?' My deputy and I were at something of a loss. 'We're not even sure where the levers are', we replied. When we thought about the question, though, we realised that the levers are all around us. Suggestions for improvement bubble up from anywhere that is appropriate. For example, in the past year our experts in learning difficulties and learning styles (we have an unusual dyslexia unit) have highlighted the need for *all* teachers to understand the individual learning styles of *all* our students, not just those with special needs. So at their suggestion, training days have been devoted to the topic and there is a cross-curricular initiative under way to teach study and learning skills explicitly within the context of individual subjects. Our heads of year wanted to help pastoral staff, the form tutors, to develop an increased range of strategies for doing pastoral work with their tutor groups, so whole-staff training was organised in Circle Time techniques.

On another occasion, a group of younger staff felt strongly that more guidance should be given on handling disciplinary incidents, and that senior staff should be checking more closely that administrative tasks were being carried out properly. I picked up these feelings from conversation with one or two of them: my way of trusting teachers to do the dull jobs had been too hands-off, and appeared as *laissez faire*. So after a range of meetings with those interested teachers (arranged, organised and minuted by that original group, so the rest of the staff could read where discussions were going, if they wanted, and even join them), new policies and practices were implemented. Now my deputy and I do indeed check more closely and this is seen (mostly) as support and awareness of what teachers do. At the same time we quickly learn if we are asking teachers to do more than they can achieve within a particular time-scale.

The 'levers of change' within the school, then, are those people (teachers or students) who see a need to do something better or differently, and who can always find a forum in which to make their views heard. Many levers for change are outside the school, of course – government or examination board initiatives, for example. In such cases, an appropriate group from among the staff will discuss the issue and plan the implementation of the school's response. This can appear fuzzy, because there is no pre-arranged hierarchical response to the need for change, but if it is fuzzy, it is also effective. The change in the pattern of Advanced (A) levels to the two-phase AS and A2, for example, has profound implications for staffing and timetabling. There have been many changes to make, and there has been no little anxiety among subject departments as to what the effect will be. So far we feel that our responses have been the right ones. They have been measured, never rushed, and never imposed. On the contrary, detailed and, at times, passionate meetings – particularly of heads of department – have talked through the issues, and asked me or other senior staff to find out further information to aid the decision making, until the appropriate solution for this school has become clear.

The same visiting inspector asked me who makes the final decisions. I had to pause. 'I do ultimately, I suppose', I said. 'But I never feel that I have to go up a mountain on my own and come back with the tablets of stone.' On the contrary, by the time any big decision has to be taken it has usually been so fully discussed that a consensus has emerged and the way forward is obvious.

It is worth mentioning, perhaps, that we do not spend hours of discussion on every issue. Indeed, one of the lessons we had to learn early on in our attempts to democratise our decision-making process was when it was worth spending time on issues, and when it was not. For example, a major decision about the implementation of a whole new pattern of post-16 examinations naturally justified and received significant hours of meeting and discussion time. On the other hand, over the years we have become quite slick at identifying issues that do not merit tying down a whole meeting. In such cases there is usually a quick consensus that a small group should go away and work on an issue and come back with a suggestion. This is likely to be simply rubber-stamped, because it will have been made with the views of others very much in mind and with informal consultation behind the scenes.

Transformational leadership and school culture

Change as a fact of life

So, if those are the mechanics of the changes we have made in my school over the ten years, what of the values that have driven those changes, and what lessons, if any, are there for school leaders in other settings?

UK schools are in a period of unprecedented change. For more than a decade, since education started to become ever more a focus of politicians' attention, the thrust from government for change has been relentless. Frequently the pace of change demanded has been unrealistic, and has put unreasonable pressure on many schools. All too often this has been led by the desire of government for statistics and for change, primarily in areas where improvement could be easily measured but which would not necessarily be the areas on which the professionals working in schools would feel they should be concentrating. But the pressure has persisted. Small wonder, then, if teachers in many schools might find the picture of change as a natural and beneficial result of a school's laudable desire for self-improvement hard to accept. But the fact that change has on many occasions been unreasonably demanded and poorly implemented does not of itself make the quest for improvement through change undesirable.

It is generally accepted nowadays that at the heart of the task of school leadership is not the maintenance of a particular style or level of achievement but the constant desire for improvement, and thus for change. The Hay McBer research into the characteristics of effective headteachers, now published on the website www.ncslonline.gov.uk of the National College for School Leadership, emphasises this fact strongly: indeed, the crucial term now widely used in discussion of school leadership is *transformational leadership*.

Changing the culture

I am convinced that the primary focus of school leaders' work – particularly but not exclusively the head – needs to be the very culture of the school. (By culture I mean not only the ethos within the school – the attitude of staff and students to the school and to its educational mission – but also the setting, the parents, wider community, advantages and difficulties in the geographical and economic area.) If there is genuinely a culture throughout the school that thirsts for improvement, then there must by definition be an acceptance of the need for change. So the transformational leader needs to ensure that the culture of the school is open to self-improvement and to the change that is necessary to achieve it. But what if that is not the culture that the newly arrived leader finds? After the much-publicised arrival and subsequent departure of a number of 'superheads' in the past few years, more thought has been given than hitherto to the importance of the culture of a school. At last some consideration is being given to the importance of school leaders having an understanding of the culture and setting of the school they are joining, and the necessity for them to work with it and within it:

> *According to Neil Burson of Leicester University Education Management Development Unit, many superheads in Fresh Start schools fail because they do not find out until too late what the stakeholders in the school and community are expecting – and that includes the pupils. 'The result is that the superhead is transferring the wrong sets of ideas and expectations to the school.'*

(Education Journal, *October 2000*)

Even if an incoming school head does fully understand the culture and can assess what aspects need to be changed, he or she can be isolated and, without sufficient support and allies, prove unable to change that culture. A moving and somewhat depressing account of such an experience was given in one of *Guardian* journalist Nick Davies's penetrating investigative articles of November 1999, now published in book form (Davies, 2000: 63–82). In a series of three articles about schools in deprived areas, Davies claimed that poverty and low educational achievement *are* inextricably linked and that politicians are simply not being honest about this. He demonstrated it beyond doubt, to my mind, and Education Secretary David Blunkett's furious response tended to substantiate that truth!

Davies then moved on to look at the independent sector. He contrasted leading independent school, Roedean, and its culture of high aspiration, self-belief and achievement, with an 11–16 school nearby on a tough estate in Brighton. Not only was the latter school in an exceptionally difficult area (the head was routinely dealing with the effects of poverty, homosexual gang-rape, drug abuse and child prostitution) but the staff were (perhaps understandably) demoralised to the point at which they had just about given up and had adopted a siege mentality. They were resistant to change, seeing it as entirely threatening, and apparently supported in, and incited to, blocking the head's attempts to turn things round by a vice-chair of governors who was an embittered former member of staff opposed to the head's appointment. Davies's story ends sadly in the head's early retirement on ill-health grounds. She could not change the culture on her own. A few things did change, and there were some grounds for optimism. But in the end the overwhelming negativity of the setting and of the culture proved too much for one person (which begs a question in itself) to change. It broke her.

Transformational leadership is to do with getting involved in the very culture of the school and moving that forward, rather than simply creating structures and mechanisms to achieve improvement. The whole school has to be prepared to change, and Davies's article demonstrates that one person alone cannot do it without support and allies. The school as a whole needs to build the capacity for change; again, this can start only at the very fundamental level of the culture and ethos of the school. The means of developing a capacity for change are succinctly described by a serving headteacher, Kate Griffin (Griffin, 2001).

How culture change is rooted in values

Walking the talk

Since starting to think about this, I have come to understand much more about how school leaders can indeed change the culture of a school. For example, heads who believe that their school should operate in a particular way would be foolish to carry out their own management tasks in a way that contradicted that approach (though one might say that such contradictions are all too frequently evident in school management). But the successful development of a school culture is something much deeper than merely ensuring executive consistency of operation.

I worked with Kate Griffin and others to produce a book (Bennett et al., 2001) in which a group of us discuss different aspects of what we choose to call *The Creativity of School Leadership*. The area that I found myself investigating was the way in which school leadership is, in effect and operation, moral leadership. School leaders are expected and seen to live their professional lives according to a set of strongly held values, principles which inform not only their professional actions but their whole lives. Such leaders are seen to walk the talk, and it is in doing so that they have the most profound effect on the prevailing culture that they have inherited and the new culture that they want to develop.

My experience illustrates this. What I have only recently come to appreciate is the extent to which walking the talk means literally that. As I have explained, when I became head I was convinced that all teachers should appear to students to be approachable. My thinking developed and I became rapidly committed to spreading democratic practice within the school, allowing students the right to a voice and to real power over their lives and learning. It is not easy to convince people about this kind of management style: people in and outside school tend to be understandably suspicious, wondering how far the commitment to consultation will go (Ginnis and Trafford, 1995: 75). In my case they suspected perhaps that it would last only until I found I was not able to get my way (always the acid test!). Similarly, students wondered whether all the talk would really make any difference, and found the pace of change too slow (Trafford, 1997: 20; Harber and Trafford, 1999: 49).

(At my first meeting) all that happened was a bunch of sixth formers messing about as soon as Mr Trafford left the room.

(Trafford, 1997: 28)

And there were comments from older students like: 'The head isn't doing anything!'

Although I think I lived up to my principle of being available and approachable, I had completely underestimated the extent to which people would simply not get around to doing the approaching! So, in my eleventh year of headship, I now try *literally* to walk the talk: to get out of the office and be about the school more than I have ever done. I attend every Student Council meeting, symbolically sitting to the right of the council's elected chair, not dominating but clearly there to hear what students have to say – to be held to account, indeed. I try to make sure that I am about in the staff room, and in support at all manner of school events and activities, because the brief informal word with colleagues (particularly if I suspect that they are troubled in some way) is far more fruitful than waiting for the trouble to brew into something that brings them up the stairs into my office. The quick chat about the activity we are supervising can easily provide an opening into the real issue.

I now do more patrolling and supervisory duties (either on an official rota or simply making sure that I am out and about) than I ever did. I blush to think how absent from those activities I was in the early years of my headship (thinking that my distance was indicative of my trust in colleagues). Nowadays, stationing myself on the corner of the busy road outside school (where students are most tempted to run across the road to catch the bus instead of using the zebra crossing), I have the opportunity for all manner of informal chat with students on their way home. Few fail to raise a smile; most will exchange a word, and sometimes more. Laughter and banter at bus stops are great ice-breakers, and serve to remind students that the head is someone to whom they can talk if and when they need to. The moral is that I realised very late just how much walking the talk meant *really* walking, being mobile, being out and about and talking to the people while on the move.

It is never too late to learn ways of improving that vital contact with teachers or students. An old friend of mine, once a colleague and now a head, showed me round his school a few years ago. I found it a humbling experience. Every student he passed greeted him warmly, and he knew everyone by name. Even though he had a visitor, an old friend, with him, he stopped and had a word with the couple of students who needed it. I went back to my own school determined to try harder to make sure that I knew names and faces. I will never be as good at it as my friend is, but by working at it I have improved – and I am sure that the ready greeting and conversation I receive from pupils is a result of my increased efforts.

It is so easy to look busy and preoccupied and walk past young people, so easy to make them feel frozen out. The same is true of colleagues. One Friday evening, I received an anxious phone call from a teacher. He had been worrying ever since the morning, afraid that he had mortally offended me in some way. The reason for this was that he had come in to use the photocopier in my secretary's office, and I had walked straight past him without speaking. I had actually been preoccupied and had barely noticed him, but he thought I was consciously ignoring him. I was mortified. Whatever the underlying reasons for that colleague's feeling so threatened, I had committed the error, unpardonable in a leader, of being too busy to notice a colleague. Since that time I have made a rule never to walk past a colleague without speaking and, if there has been some disagreement between us, to try all the more to ensure that a pleasantry is exchanged – just so we both know that there is no estrangement between us.

How we change the culture in practice

Earlier, I described one of the elements of the culture of a school, its ethos, as being the attitude of teachers and students to the school and their perception of its purpose. Yet the purpose of a school is often described as its *vision*, and it has long been expected that school leaders must have a clear vision for the school. My contention is that the vital vision must be rooted in the culture, be sensitive to it (and possibly to its shortcomings), and that the vision must include both aspirations and strategies for moulding the culture, indeed for transforming it. So transformational leadership starts with the leader (and leadership group) having a clear vision which is rooted in the reality of the setting. And then through articulation of that vision – and also through negotiation, argument and persuasion – school leaders have to move that culture forward, taking account of fears and sensitivities, and understanding that the aspirations of parents, students and teachers might be very different in one area than in another. Only from that point can effective and lasting transformation begin. This aspect of school leadership is of incomparably greater importance as a first step than putting measurement or assessment mechanisms in place, setting targets, changing classroom practice and the like. Those features are symptoms of how a school works, not causes of it. We have to start with fundamentals, and they are rooted in the culture.

One of my early mechanisms for involving staff in policy planning was to set up a think-tank. This had open membership, as do most of our working groups, but I specifically invited one or two colleagues to ensure that there was a good representation of old hands and new arrivals, of senior and comparatively junior staff. The think-tank met initially with an open brief to decide what it ought to think about, though we had already shared concerns about students taking responsibility for their learning and behaviour, so that there were already items on the agenda. Very rapidly, though, the group came to the conclusion that we should not try to deal with any of these issues until we had first looked at defining the central purpose and aims of the school.

The setting of the school is very particular, which is why clarification and definition of purpose were so necessary; but perhaps that is true of *every* school. Mine is a former town boys' grammar school, now independent and co-educational, still academically selective but totally committed to widening access rather than narrowing it, to providing the broadest education to students, and to valuing involvement and high standards of achievement outside the classroom just as much as inside it. At the time when I became head, the school had survived a decade of independence. It was still establishing its new position in the town and area; defining its constituency of support among parents and potential students; working out its relationship with a Labour-controlled local authority that had inevitably been hostile to its move into independence; finding its feet in an area beset by recession and the loss of its traditional base of heavy industry; and planning for the introduction of co-education. The need to clarify its aims was palpable. A traditional grammar school will tend to have a culture of high expectation and high achievement, but (as I wrote earlier) when I became head in 1990 a great many of the staff were concerned that the level of commitment from students was simply not high enough. So even the 'simple' academic aim needed a clearer focus.

The process was fascinating. We constantly narrowed the focus until we had decided on key words that encapsulated what we felt this school in particular focused upon. From these key concepts (identified below by underlining) came the following succinct statement which we call the school philosophy, but which could equally well be described as a mission statement:

The Challenge of Scholarship

The Spirit of Commitment

The philosophy of Wolverhampton Grammar School places <u>scholarship</u> at the heart of a <u>challenging</u> education which promotes achievement through <u>active involvement</u>. It seeks to develop <u>self-awareness</u> and a sense of <u>responsibility</u>, values both <u>individuality</u> and <u>altruism</u>, and fosters the <u>spirit of community and commitment</u> traditional to the School.

Eight years later, we still use the same philosophy, unchanged, as our mission statement. It is followed, in most public statements, by a single page of explanation of what we think these key ideas should mean to our students, and with some notes for parents too. Having succeeded in encapsulating the school's overriding purpose and aims into that short statement, the task of relating other concerns and new developments to the core purpose became a great deal easier. As quite radical changes have taken place in the school over the years, it has always been possible to reassure those who are nervous of change that the philosophy, the central aim of the school, remains unaltered. This serves both as reassurance and as a reminder of the primary focus of the school.

Throughout the school's publications and policy documents, the concept of the spirit of commitment is constantly reiterated. This is partly a conscious attempt to combat the 'three-minute culture' with which it appears all schools have to contend at present. It is a truism that young people who want to achieve significantly need to make a real commitment of time and effort to do so; yet this is not the message all too frequently portrayed in media stories of get-rich-quick and instant gratification. Hence this emphasis on commitment. To be sure, my influence is to be seen: following the Bellman in Lewis Caroll's *The Hunting of the Snark*, I tend to operate on the basis that 'what I say three times is true'! In a sense, this reiterates my earlier point about the need for school leaders to persuade and cajole. We have to proselytise tirelessly. The message does get over, however, and the culture does change – but nothing happens quickly.

Qualities: the link between values and functions

How the leader's personal qualities link vision, culture and day-to-day routines

In a paper about values and moral leadership (Trafford, 2001), I proposed that between the building bricks of the underlying values that drive a school leader's moral leadership and those of the everyday management functions, the nuts and bolts of the job, there needs to be mortar, something softer that binds them all together. Forming that mortar, I identified primary qualities which I believed to be essential to school leaders. These qualities are, I believe, what tie school leaders' values into their everyday work. In those qualities that they bring to their work they consistently link their principles both to the long-term task of developing and transforming the culture and to the immediate routines of running the school day by day.

Inevitably, all of us possess these qualities in different proportions and will certainly find that we are lacking in some of them. The purpose of my paper was to suggest that, if we work at mapping them, we should be able to create ways of helping school leaders, and potential leaders, to develop those qualities in which they feel less confident. As I explored these ideas, and started listing and connecting the kind of qualities on which school leaders have to draw every day of their professional lives, I found two things. First, the list keeps growing every time I look at it. Second, I found that:

There is in effect a hierarchy of qualities, since one tends to grow out of another; passion, courage and sensitivity.

From passion *flow*

- *charisma*
- *creativity*

While courage *gives rise to*

- *humility*
- *confidence*
- *self-awareness*
- *emotional maturity*
- *self-belief*
- *self-knowledge*
- *judgement*
- *patience.*

In the interpersonal sphere, sensitivity *might be seen to give rise to*

- *empathy*
- *vulnerability*
- *tolerance.*

(Trafford, 2001)

These qualities operate and interact in a very complex manner. Indeed, if school leaders had to think consciously about the extent and proportion to which they needed to bring them into play in every situation, they would soon get bogged down. Fortunately, we tend to draw on them unconsciously most of the time. This does not mean that we should be unaware of them, though, nor that in preparation for, or refreshment of, school leadership we should not devote significant amounts of time to thinking about them. In that same paper I identified ways in which potential school leaders should be encouraged to map their personal development plan of values and qualities.

These qualities are vital, because the teachers and students who interact with school leaders look for moral leadership and see the qualities of the leader in action long before the results of his or her actions become discernible. Quick-fix solutions to problems can bring about rapid change, but lasting and sustainable change and improvement, *transformation*, take time. Leaders have to be able to convince those with a stake in the change that its results, when noticeable, will have been worth waiting for. In the meantime, though, they will need to trust – and people will only trust a leader who is visibly committed to the institution and the people in it, and who clearly believes in the mission.

Explaining, persuading – and losing arguments

It is for this reason that I stress that the vision must be made real by the way in which the leader lives it. Notwithstanding what I wrote above, 'walking the talk' is about more than just being visible and approachable. Leaders who clearly 'know the theory' but pass it on as something learned and second-hand do not achieve lasting change, however mobile they are. They are not believed. Those who clearly believe in the vision, and articulate it passionately, *are* believed, however – and rightly so. Hence the emphasis on the term *passionate leadership* and the rightness of Howard Gardner's (1996) identification of two sorts of leader (among others): the storyteller – who persuades and inspires – and the expert – the lead professional. Gardner describes them as two different leadership styles, because there are ways in which one style weakens the other if both are adopted. But school leaders are expected precisely to play the two parts at once, illustrating once again the complexity of the role. I can remember times when, arguing for a particular development, I have said in some frustration: 'Look, I know about this.' Of course, I was losing the battle if I had to lay claim to knowledge instead of simply demonstrating it. With the 'expert' must come Gardner's 'storyteller' who, with passion and charisma, encourages, persuades and helps others to find creative solutions.

Storytellers can be hurt when the audience is not sympathetic. My experience is of bitter hurt at times when I felt that my attempts to move things forward were misunderstood or misinterpreted, often, as it seemed, by selfish interests or deliberate attempts to undermine. When the sincerity of our motives, of our vision for the school, is questioned, our confidence takes a severe knock. My full account of making changes in my school mentions a particularly bleak entry in the diary I kept for research purposes:

> *I am still unhappy and rather on edge and in one of my all-too-frequent moods in which I would like to chuck it all up if I could.*

> (Trafford, 1997: 61)

I mentioned earlier that I was sensitive (probably over-sensitive) to criticism, particularly of the more ungenerous sort. I have certainly developed a thicker skin over the past decade, and am less frequently hurt, though there are still dark days when I go home in the depths of gloom and spread a pall of misery over hearth and family. This is not entirely negative, though it undoubtedly (and unfairly) tries the patience of my wife and children; at least we do not have a cat for me to kick! School leaders must not develop so thick a skin that nothing touches them deeply; we rightly criticise the kind of leaders who, in their insecurity, erect barriers (of status, style, procedure, manner, furniture, location) to keep people at a distance. There are a host of strategies that defensive leaders can (and do) use to protect themselves. But the sensitivity that allows us to be hurt at times is vital if we are also to be sensitive to the needs and fears of others in school, and to tolerate their foibles, their views that do not accord with ours, and even their mistakes.

> *Sensitivity, the ability to be touched or even wounded, is an essential quality for school leaders. As a colleague recently told me, 'When I forget my vulnerability is when I start to make inhuman decisions'.*
>
> *(Trafford, 2001)*

Conflict hurts. In managing any organisation, however small or simple, there will be conflicts from time to time. The task of leading schools is fraught with them. Despite the National Curriculum and performance data that may appear to move the work of schools towards uniformity, there are so many personal aspirations and frustrations involved, so many different aims and goals and so few hard and measurable outcomes. No two people want the same from education for themselves, their pupils or their children except in the most general terms. And all the people involved in schools – students, parents, teachers, the local community – are themselves growing and developing all the time, so their hopes and desires are constantly shifting. Somehow the team leading a school has to harness all those energies, try to neutralise or reroute those that act against the desired general direction for the school, and lead everyone, like the American pioneers of old, towards a new land that they have not seen but which they have been persuaded will be better. Ways in which that might be achieved have been described earlier.

Courage to keep going

But what of the leaders themselves? How do they find refreshment and encouragement? Some comes from the principles and values that drive them, their sense of mission. But that can wear thin by Friday evening towards the end of a long term. At that stage different leaders find different ways of coping. Many swim or jog. I am amazed (or, more truthfully, shamed) by how many colleagues at a conference will dash off at the end of the day's sessions to take some serious exercise before dinner; presumably they do that at home too. I am afraid I am one of those who head straight for the bar, though not without a twinge of guilt that I have once again failed to hit my target of going cycling three times a week.

Therapeutic though exercise or even drinking with friends can be (though the after-effects of the two activities are quite different), they are, up to a point, avoidance strategies. In the end, the difficulties of our job as school leaders have to be faced. And facing up to anything hard takes courage. Courage as a quality essential in school leaders may be defined in many ways:

- courage to express, and to be challenged on, deeply held personal convictions;
- courage to tell the truth when it is unpalatable or unpopular and to remain silent when the truth would hurt needlessly;
- courage to compromise, even on principle, in order to build consensus; to 'agree to agree' to others' convictions; to work as part of a team; to adopt the 'female' (consensual) style of management rather than the macho (confrontational) style;
- courage to accept and face conflict when consensus or compromise cannot be achieved; to confront wrong or injustice without backing down; to step in to protect teachers or students from abuse or aggression; to accept the loneliness of doing what is right;
- courage to trust others to innovate, experiment and take risks; to accept the sacrifice of direct control and the proportion of failure that may result; to devolve power to teachers and students and allow them to grow as independent, self-reliant people;
- courage to aim for self-knowledge and understanding of one's emotional growth in order to analyse one's successes or difficulties;
- humility to accept guidance and to admit mistakes;
- confidence in one's judgement;
- confidence to shed status and meet others (including students) on equal terms;
- confidence to move on from disappointment or failure to the next challenge; to refuse to be overwhelmed by routines or bureaucracy and keep one's eye instead on the 'big picture';
- judgement; the ability to make decisions based on experience, knowledge and an understanding of one's reaction and motives, and of other people's;
- patience to accept the loss of small battles in the context of the larger campaign; to refuse to be stampeded into important decisions; to keep a sense of humour and use laughter as a more effective response than anger or anguish.

(Trafford, 2001)

Courage is needed in the bad times. On the days when we go home in black despair, as I certainly do, we need confidence in our overall vision to put things in perspective; to decide that we have only lost one battle in a much longer struggle; that we did not handle the situation as well as we could have and that we can try to retrieve matters tomorrow; that we shall have to eat humble pie, admit our error and make amends; that we *were* right, despite appearances, and cannot back down on this point of principle; that what felt like an attack on us personally was far more an expression of the other person's internal turmoil and anger; that in the end it was not a big issue, and it is our pride that has been hurt, not our competence. It is easy to write such apparently wise and balanced judgements, but much harder to think through them at the difficult times.

I have a little personal rule that helps me through those times when someone appears in the office, usually late in the week and term, and unloads their feelings about how they or their child are undervalued and unfairly treated, how the school and (explicitly or by implication) my management are failing dismally and blighting their lives. As the one-sided tirade progresses, and I resolutely remind myself that my open-door policy encourages this sort of disclosure and that *it is a good thing*, even on a Friday, a feeling of depression settles on me. 'Am I really getting it all *so* wrong?' I wonder. Then a small voice whispers in my head, 'One of us is barmy, and I don't think it's me'. At that moment the other person will invariably say something so biased or incorrect that I am immediately reassured that it is an entirely one-sided view that is being presented. It sounds smug, perhaps, but this *does* happen time after time, and at such moments I say to myself, 'Ah, yes: the rule has proved itself again'.

At the end they usually say, 'Well, I feel better now!' as the burden is shifted, for the moment, from their shoulders to mine. But the burden is bearable now; the voice has whispered its message to me and the balance is restored. The whole thing is not disastrous even if one person is discontented. I may not be completely right and the feeling of grievance may be justified so that I know I must do something about it, but I know I am not totally in the wrong, either. I can begin to negotiate a way through. Somewhere at the bottom of this, I think, lie the self-knowledge and judgement born of experience that allow me to regain a sense of perspective – and confidence. The exchange may not have been pleasurable, but at the end it is not wholly demoralising either, and sometimes a positive rapprochement can be attempted.

Promoting courage in others: trusting and delegating power

Much of my decade of headship has, as I have described, been involved in trying to shed power and give responsibility to others, both in order to enable them to grow as individuals and because they know better than I how to do their job as teacher – or student. I am convinced that the power of the school leader is to empower and instil confidence in others, not to appear powerful. Transformational school leadership is concerned with moving the entire school culture towards a desire and capability for change and improvement. Change is sustainable only when everyone, or at least the overwhelming majority of participants, is committed to it and involved in it. There has to be ownership of the improvement by all. The best leaders thus devolve power, rather than wield it. Delegation and devolution need courage. It takes courage to trust others to run things: part of the leader's task is also to pass on confidence to those who accept that devolved power.

The famous dictum of Taoist philosopher Lao Tse is never truer than in schools: 'Of the best leader, the people will say, "We did it ourselves".'

School leaders frequently have to promote confidence and courage in their teachers. There are so many pressures from outside school that teachers need enormous amounts of reassurance. Not only are curricular change and new initiatives constants nowadays, but monitoring, benchmarking and inspection systems are so demanding as to be perceived as hostile, whatever the intentions of those who set them up. Legal issues, once the real concern only of the head, now worry teachers profoundly. Everywhere we see evidence that teachers are becoming less willing to be involved in sporting, outdoor or even classroom and playground activities that bear an element of risk. The threat of litigation is potent, and the fear of professional ruin tangible.

> *Playground games such as skipping and rounders are being banned by primary headteachers who fear that they will be sued by parents or criticised by inspectors if children are injured.*
>
> *Some schools have also outlawed conkers, claiming that they are 'offensive weapons', and football is often forbidden because it is considered anti-social.*
>
> *(Budge and Kirkman, 2000)*

I guess most right-minded parents and teachers would deplore the demise of such playground games. The article quoted above is yet another demonstration of the need for courage and confidence in schools, and in those who lead them.

Courage is thus both an internal and an external quality. It is a truism that if leaders are to be 'followable' they need to display confidence. If they are to display confidence they need (mostly, at any rate) to *feel* confident. I have already mentioned the danger, indeed the unacceptability, of leaders putting on a front or erecting barriers to protect themselves. True confidence comes from self-knowledge, from understanding ourselves, our strengths *and* our weaknesses. The better we understand ourselves, the better able we are to overcome or compensate for our weaknesses, the better we can stand up and play the leadership role, and the easier it is to be brave.

Conclusion: what school leaders do, and how they can learn to do it

So, if all the people in schools are to espouse the cause of constant improvement and accept the need for change in order to achieve it, leaders are confronting an immensely complex task. They articulate and live the vision. They set the tone and communicate it. They display and promote the qualities needed. They set the example. They must, if the courage, confidence, judgement, humility, sensitivity and passion they display are to be replicated throughout the school. And if all the participants are to take their share of responsibility for the school's progress and achievement, they must be replicated not just in those aspiring to take on more senior positions but in everyone, including the students. When things get difficult, school leaders have to be both the steady, reassuring hand on the tiller and the buffer that absorbs the pressure from outside. They have both to push and to be leaned on. And they have to refresh and reinforce themselves while encouraging and reinvigorating others.

This is the burdensome yet uniquely stimulating task of moral leadership in the school setting. The quotation from Irene Dalton with which I began, sums up both the strengths and the immense demands of the role, and Hay McBer's research serves to reinforce her view:

> *Russell Hobby, project manager of Hay McBer's education division, said: 'This study contains a very positive message. In general, there is a great deal of strong, versatile leadership in our schools.'*

> *(Kelly, 2000)*

There needs to be. It is in the personal and interpersonal nature of the role, not in the ability to handle myriad managerial and mechanical functions, that the role is so unusual and so tough. But it is do-able. None of us is good at *all* of it – but Hay McBer and Dalton alike suggest, to my mind, that leading successful schools there are people who are *good enough at enough of the many facets* of the job to make it work.

I am convinced that the key to successful school leadership lies in the development of the appropriate personal qualities in potential leaders. However, there is still a need for more research into this bewildering range of qualities, into how they make for effective leaders and how they might be developed in individuals who aspire to leadership roles in education. It is my hope, explained in depth elsewhere (Trafford, 2001), that our new National College for School Leadership will recognise that complexity more than anyone has hitherto. All teachers are leaders, to a greater or lesser degree, so all need to be aware of the nature and constituent elements of moral leadership. I hope we shall see training and self-development programmes along these lines for all teachers so that, from the moment of entry to the profession (and indeed before it), they begin to address the intangible yet vital areas of qualities and values.

Such training will not be easy, nor will it be quick. That is not the nature of the job, so we should not expect training or solutions to be quick. Indeed, they should match the job itself. As Dalton (2000) concludes:

> *No short cuts. No sound bites. School leadership is not rhetoric but lived out, quietly, day by day.*

Therein lie the strength, the uniqueness and the challenge of school leadership – and thus of preparation for it. It is an exciting challenge, though, and I, for one, am prepared to accept it.

References

Bennett, D., Clough, J., Cox, K., Griffin, K. and Trafford, B. (2001) *The Creativity of School Leadership*. Leicester: Secondary Heads Association.

Blishen, E. (ed.) (1969) *The School That I'd Like*. London: Penguin Books.

Budge, D. and Kirkman, S. (2000) 'Skipping banned in safety drive' in *Times Educational Supplement*, 8 December.

Dalton, I. (2000) 'Holding the line' editorial in *Headlines* (journal of the Secondary Heads Association), 34, November.

Davies, N. (2000) *The School Report: Why Britain's Schools Are Failing*. London: Vintage.

Gardner, H. (1996) *Leading Minds: An Anatomy of Leadership*. London: HarperCollins.

Ginnis, P. and Trafford, B. (1995) 'Headteachers and the challenge of choosing democracy' in Harber, C. (ed.) *Developing Democratic Education*. Ticknall: Education Now Books.

Griffin, K. (2001) 'Building the capacity for change' in Bennett, D. et al.; op.cit.

Harber, C. and Meighan, R. (eds) (1989) *The Democratic School*. Ticknall: Education Now Books.

Harber, C. and Trafford, B. (1999) 'Democratic management and school effectiveness in two countries: a case of pupil participation?' in *Educational Management and Administration*, 27 (1) 45–54.

Kelly, A. (2000) 'Heads outperform captains of industry' in *Times Educational Supplement*, 8 December.

Meighan, R. (1986) *A Sociology of Educating*. London, Cassell [new edition: Meighan, R. and Siraj-Blatchford, I. (2000) *Sociology of Educating*. London: Continuum Publishing Group].

Trafford, B. (1997) *Participation, Power-sharing and School Improvement*. Nottingham: Educational Heretics Press.

Trafford, B. (2000) 'Much more than soggy chips' in *Headlines* (journal of the Secondary Heads Association), 34, November.

Trafford, B. (2001) 'Values, qualities and moral leadership' in Bennett, D et al., op.cit.

2

■ ■ ■

Learning To Learn – Engaging the 10 Per Cent

by Tony Hinkley

Learning is the most powerful, engaging, rewarding and enjoyable aspect of our personal and collective experience. The ability to learn about learning and become masters of the learning process is the critical issue for the next century.

(Honey, 1999)

Why 'learning to learn'?

Do schools really provide an education for their pupils or do they largely teach them to pass the examinations necessary for their first steps into the big wide world? I hope that today no one would accept that a merely utilitarian view of schools is an acceptable one, even though the 'back to basics' lobby might disagree. Most recent initiatives from government could be described as a major push to raise standards. Who can argue with the measured increase in attainment that is evident as a consequence of these approaches? These initiatives are well documented but can take us only so far in raising standards. If we are to achieve a truly 'world-class' education system, we need to look beyond the 'standards agenda' and into research that looks at how learning best takes place. Measuring a school (or government) by exam result indicators is easy. However, just because we can measure something does not make it important and, equally, being unable to measure something does not make it unimportant.

Our priorities have to be clear. Education is more than the standards agenda, important as this undoubtedly is. It is encouraging that we are now seeing government recognise this – but what is this new view of the world of education and how does it complement the work already begun in raising standards? Given that the world is a rapidly changing place, that the pace of change is ever increasing and that coping with this increasing pace of change is potentially very stressful, how do we prepare pupils to live in a world we have not experienced?

Our education systems (and our schools) were designed for a time and purpose that no longer exist. John West-Burnham encapsulated this premise when he wrote:

> There are many clichés about 20th-century teachers in 19th-century institutions preparing young people for the 21st century but in essence it is very difficult to find an educational justification for the way in which most schools organise the student experience. The use of time (periods, days, terms, years) has only limited relationship to learning but a lot to do with control. The use of space (classrooms and so on) is largely derived from an otherwise discredited monitorial system.

(West-Burnham, 2000)

The concept of a job for life is now the exception rather than the rule, though here, perhaps, teaching is the major exception. Most young people in our schools today will experience what is known as 'portfolio careers' – moving on, not just through several companies but through several careers, including jobs which do not even exist yet. For example, how many of us were given careers advice at school about becoming, say, a website designer? Skills are developmental and transferable. Positive attitudes of mind and adaptability make the unknown a challenge to be welcomed rather than a future to be feared.

With all of this uncertainty, curriculum design that is rooted in subject content becomes increasingly and rapidly outdated and immaterial to students' real and future needs. Learning how to learn becomes the key to coping. Our rapidly developing understanding of how learning takes place challenges the current structural paradigm of schools and traditional pedagogy. The emergence of research findings in neuro-science, recent developments in cognitive psychology and the success of new models of learning add weight to the criticism of the compartmentalised experience of most students in secondary education.

In accepting this premise, learning as a topic will supersede all others. Indeed, the right to learn and the right to be helped in developing one's skills as a learner must be an inalienable right for all people. Similarly, the task of developing these skills in people must be seen as one of the most rewarding career options for young people. Our society must play its part in valuing and respecting this 'new' profession of teacher, and politicians also have their part to play.

Learning is a skill which, like any other skill, can be developed and improved. Learning to learn must, therefore, become the ultimate life skill and have the understanding and status it deserves. This focus on learning is not divorced from standards – learning to learn translates into improved performance, but persists beyond any examination or assessment.

Guy Claxton (2000) of Bristol University describes three levels of learning to learn. The first is improved performance of the individual student (for example, examination practice). Level 2 he describes as learning to learn for school and this might include the teaching of study skills, thus contributing to improving learners in a school, resulting in improved standards. Level 3 is learning to learn for life. At this level students are helped to develop the positive attitudes of mind that enable them to cope with what Claxton calls life's 'complex uncertainties'.

Each of these described levels has value in making its own contribution to improved standards. Each level offers something different and adds to the previous one in terms of sustained engagement with life's complexities and challenges. It is clear to me that we should be absolutely convinced that learning is learnable. Therefore, we should no longer think about difficulty with a task in terms of a lack of ability, but more as an opportunity to explore appropriate learning approaches in order to succeed.

Clearly, teachers will have a different role in this new paradigm, and one that many have not been trained for. Teachers will become experts in developing pupils as learners as well as (or instead of?) experts delivering content. One of the core areas in our curriculum ought to be a response to the question of what it means to be a strong learner. We can look forward to the day when 'learnacy' (Guy Claxton's term) will take its rightful place alongside literacy and numeracy in the government's thinking.

Of course, these ideas go beyond the years of compulsory schooling. Could it be argued, as Ian Gilbert (2000) has said, that a qualification-centred education is doing young people a disservice as we help them prepare for work? In a world of unceasing change, where yesterday's answers no longer fit today's problems and knowledge is doubling at an ever-increasing rate, life-long learning is the only way forward for our society. Qualifications will get you a good job, but only when backed up by positive attitudes, because time and time again we see that qualifications alone are not enough.

What has history told us?

Alfred Binet is usually given the honour of having introduced the world to intelligence tests. In the early 1900s, as families were flocking to Paris from the provinces and elsewhere, it was observed that some of the children from these families were having great difficulty with schoolwork. Binet was approached by the Ministry of Education in France to help predict which children were at risk of failure at school. He administered hundreds of test questions to these children, wanting to identify a set of questions that, when passed, predicted success in school and when failed, predicted difficulty.

The Intelligence Quotient (IQ) test then made its way across the Atlantic to America. From being a one-to-one test it became a test that could be administered to large numbers through paper and pencil. By the mid-1920s the intelligence test had become a relatively inexpensive and 'easy to apply' fixture in educational practice in the USA and it remained with us in the western world until recent times. Following Binet's example, intelligence tests since then have been heavily weighted towards measuring in the domains of verbal memory, verbal reasoning, numerical reasoning, logical sequencing and problem solving.

Much later, in 1983, Howard Gardner published the first of his books on Multiple Intelligences. In contrast to Binet, Gardner argued that it is wrong to assume that IQ is a single, fixed, measurable entity. He argued that instead of asking 'how smart are you?' we ought to be asking 'how are you smart?'.

Gardner defined intelligence as 'an ability to solve a problem or fashion a product that is valued in one or more cultural settings'. He outlined seven intelligences, to which he later added an eighth. The first seven were:

- linguistic: a facility with language, patterning and systems;
- mathematical/logical: likes precision, enjoys abstract thinking, likes structure and order;
- visual/spatial: thinks in pictures and mental images, good with maps, charts and diagrams, uses movement to assist learning;
- musical: sensitive to mood and emotion, enjoys rhythm, turned on by music and affected by it;
- kinaesthetic: uses body skilfully, good at timing, likes to act out ideas and touch, good control of objects;
- interpersonal: relates well to others, good communicator, mediates, enjoys working in groups;
- intrapersonal: reflects on personal traits and attitudes.

The later addition was:

- naturalistic: ability to make connections in the natural world, understands the living world, drawn to ecological issues, enjoys learning within context rather than out of context.

In 2000 Danah Zohar published *Connecting With Our Spiritual Intelligence*, in which she argues that this is the most powerful intelligence we possess. She asserts that it is through our spiritual intelligence that we make meaning out of our lives, touching our deepest and most profound core principles. Spiritual intelligence is where our passion for learning comes from and is where our most creative thinking will emerge (if we cultivate it). Gardner, too, is now exploring a ninth – existential or spiritual – intelligence, thus demonstrating that we are all learners and that learning is a continuous activity.

Neuroscience is the study of the human nervous system, the brain, and the biological basis of consciousness, perception, memory and learning. The nervous system and the brain are the physical foundation of the human learning process. Neuroscience links our observations about cognitive behaviour with the actual physical processes that support such behaviour.

Some of the key findings of neuroscience include the work of Roger Sperry (1974) for which he received the Nobel prize in 1981. Sperry investigated the structure and functions of the brain and showed that the two different sides (hemispheres) control two different 'modes' of thinking. He also suggested that each of us has a preferred mode of operation, with a dominance of either the left-brain or right-brain thinking over the other. The left brain is concerned especially with logical, sequential, analytical, objective activity and is typified stereotypically in a scientist or mathematician. Right-brain thinkers exhibit more intuitive behaviour with a more subjective, holistic, synthesising approach. The left and right hemispheres are joined via the corpus callosum (larger in females than males), thus allowing, it is said, the right hemisphere to make sense of the pattern making of the left hemisphere.

Most individuals have a distinct preference for one of these styles of thinking. Some, however, are more whole-brained and equally adept at both modes. In schools, left-brain subjects focus on logical thinking, analysis and accuracy; right-brained subjects, on the other hand, focus on aesthetics, feeling and creativity. Is it any surprise that, historically, schools have tended to favour left-brain modes of thinking, while downplaying the right-brain ones?

In order to be more 'whole-brained' in their orientation, schools need to give equal weight to the arts, creativity, and the skills of imagination and synthesis. This is more than simply putting these subjects on the timetable (though that would be, indeed, a start in some schools). The concepts need to be understood, internalised and made explicit in curriculum design and delivery.

Teaching, therefore, needs to foster a more whole-brained educational experience for students. Teachers should use techniques that connect with both sides of the brain. Left-brain activities based on a logical and systematic approach are relatively easy to imagine and design. Teachers can increase their classroom's right-brain learning activities by incorporating more visuals, metaphors, analogies, role-playing and movement into their reading and analytical activities. This represents a different but important pedagogical shift in order to maximise the potential of students.

Paul Maclean (1983) postulated that the human brain is, in fact, made up of three brains. The most primitive of these (in behavioural and evolutionary terms) is known as the reptilian brain. This is believed to control basic sensory motor functions such as breathing and balance, and the territorial aspects of friendship and personal space. Behavioural aspects rooted here include rote behaviours such as predictable and repetitive situations, and others include attention seeking, showing off, peer identification and the useful 'flight or fight' response.

The second brain is the middle brain, also know as the mammalian or limbic brain. This powerful area controls the emotions, long-term memory and bio-rhythms. The limbic system acts as an 'emotional gatekeeper' to learning and is concerned with validation of learning and values. The third, and most advanced brain, is the neocortex or thinking brain that controls cognition, reasoning, language and higher intelligence. It is this that distinguishes us from other animals, including other primates, in terms of our higher-order reasoning skills.

Research suggests that the brain is not like a computer. The structure of the brain's neurone connections is loose, flexible, 'webbed' and overlapping, unlike the tight, ordered, predictable, linear or parallel structure of computers. As a result, the brain is better described as a self-organising system. Similarly, the brain is not a fixed entity like a computer but changes with use throughout our lifetime. Mental concentration and effort alters the physical structure of the brain (hence the 'use it or lose it' concept). Nerve cells (neurones) are connected to each other and communicate via branches called dendrites. There are about 10 billion neurones in the brain and about 1000 trillion connections. The possible number of combinations of connections is about ten to the one-millionth power. As we use the brain, we strengthen certain patterns of connection, making each connection easier to create next time. This is how memory develops.

In a report on the state of emotional literacy in the USA, Daniel Goleman stated:

> *In navigating our lives, it is our fears and envies, our rages and depressions, our worries and anxieties that steer us day to day. Even the most academically brilliant among us are vulnerable to being undone by unruly emotions. The price we pay for emotional literacy is in failed marriages and troubled families, in stunted social and work lives, in deteriorating physical health and mental anguish and, as a society, in tragedies such as killings.*

> *(Goleman, 1995)*

Goleman attests that the best remedy for fighting our emotional shortcomings is preventive medicine. In other words, we need to place as much importance on teaching our children the essential skills associated with emotional intelligence (known as EQ) as we do on more traditional 'measures' of intelligence such as IQ.

What is emotional intelligence? Goleman's concept of EQ encompasses the following five characteristics and abilities:

- self-awareness – knowing your emotions, recognising feelings as they occur, and discriminating between them;
- mood management – handling feelings so they are relevant to the current situation and you react appropriately;
- self-motivation – 'gathering up' your feelings and directing yourself towards a goal despite self-doubt, inertia and impulsiveness;

- empathy – recognising feelings in others and tuning into their verbal and non-verbal cues;
- managing relationships – handling interpersonal interaction, conflict resolution and negotiations.

Research suggests that emotional health is fundamental to effective learning. For example, Goleman (1995) states that a report in the USA concluded that the most critical element for a student's success in school is an understanding of how to learn. Is this really such a surprise? Yet how much of what we plan and do takes account of this rather obvious conclusion?

It has been shown that a student who learns how to learn is much more likely to succeed. In the USA, emotional intelligence has been demonstrated to be a better predictor of success than traditional methods such as IQ and standardised test scores. Hence the great interest in emotional intelligence on the part of corporations, universities and schools. The idea of emotional intelligence has inspired research and curriculum development and, in addition, researchers have concluded that people who manage their feelings well and deal effectively with others are more likely to live content lives. Similarly, satisfied people are more apt to retain information and do so more effectively than dissatisfied people.

Building one's emotional intelligence has a life-long impact. Many parents and educators in the USA, alarmed by increasing levels of conflict in young schoolchildren, are rushing to teach students the skills necessary to capitalise on their emotional intelligence. In corporations, it is believed that the inclusion of emotional intelligence in training programmes has helped employees co-operate better, thereby helping to increase productivity and profits.

Goleman (1995) presents a cogent argument for cultivating emotional intelligence and 'emotional literacy' in schools. He argues that the development of this under-recognised intelligence will have more of an effect on a young person's long-term success in life than a focus on cognitive intelligence.

Other work includes an exploration of the three main modes of learning, or learning styles – visual, auditory and kinaesthetic. Many teachers are now designing curriculum experiences around these three styles, thus maximising the learning potential of the students in their classes. There are areas such as the impact of diet and health on learning that have yet to be explored fully and published widely. We must continue to lead the learning in our quest to enhance autonomy in the learners in our care.

The current paradigm and looking ahead

Encouragingly, there is a very clear affirmation that the inclusion of thinking skills is a central feature in the Labour government's policies. Michael Barber, Head of the Standards and Effectiveness Unit, DfEE, and David Blunkett are keen to see this area developed and are basing their policy on research and current good practice. However, the background research provides little comfort to many teachers. This research relies heavily on Office for Standards in Education (Ofsted) data, research by Paul Black and Dylan Wiliam of King's College, London (1998) and the more recent work of Maurice Galton, John Gray and Jean Ruddock (1999) in their work commissioned by the Department for Education and Employment (DfEE) which looks at the transition from Key Stage 2 to Key Stage 3.

Ofsted evidence indicates that there is more teaching that can be described as unsatisfactory in Key Stage 3 than in any other key stage. Similarly, there is a higher proportion of teachers teaching outside their subject specialism in this key stage. Galton, Gray and Ruddock (1999) contend that many pupils are faced with work that is repetitive and unchallenging compared with their previous experience and that they do not make sufficient progress.

Research into assessment for learning (formerly called formative assessment) by Black and Wiliam (1998) found that:

- active involvement of pupils in their own learning is beneficial;
- assessment for learning has a positive influence on motivation and self-esteem;
- there is a need for pupils to assess themselves and understand how to improve;
- these approaches can improve achievement by one to two General Certificate of Secondary Education (GCSE) grades.

Ofsted is already looking for evidence of assessment for learning when it inspects schools. The inclusion of approaches to thinking skills will be introduced into a future Ofsted framework.

In addition, those involved in the Cognitive Acceleration through Science Education (CASE) programme, now used in many British schools, have noted improvements such as:

- an increase in GCSE performance by one grade, two to three years after the programme ends (i.e. the benefits are sustained);
- 19 per cent more pupils achieve A*–C in science;
- 15 per cent more pupils achieve A*–C in mathematics;
- 16 per cent more pupils achieve A*–C in English;
- the percentage achieving Level 6 at Key Stage 3 doubled.

The evidence is mounting and, thankfully, the government is listening. There is no quick fix, but we need to embed the necessary skills in primary and early secondary years and then build on them systematically. Clearly there is a need to get pupils to understand how someone assesses, as well as to get teachers to understand how pupils learn. Perhaps the really encouraging sign is the inclusion of thinking skills in the National Curriculum by the Qualification and Curriculum Authority (QCA). Thinking skills can be defined as strategies to help pupils manage their own learning. In the National Curriculum these are listed as information processing, reasoning, enquiry, creative thinking and evaluation, and should be embedded throughout the curriculum.

Interim findings from the two-year national pilot of Key Stage 3 will roll out to all schools in September 2001 (before completion or full evaluation of the project). Issues in the pilot include a recognition of the overlap between thinking skills and assessment for learning, and the acceptance that professional development is needed to embed thinking skills in the curriculum and in schemes of work. It is hoped that the findings will lead to a consistent pedagogy applicable to teaching.

The research findings of Galton, Gray and Ruddock (1999) describe some obvious and some worrying issues, including:

- 40 per cent of pupils show loss of progress or no progress on transfer to secondary school; this is related to decrease in motivation;
- work in Year 7 and Year 8 is repetitive, unchallenging and lacking purpose according to children; there is little connection with later achievement;
- peer pressure and friendship patterns are important factors and pupils recognise the difficulty for them to change due to peer expectations;
- pupil enjoyment drops in English, mathematics and science – least in English and most in science;
- science teaching is characterised by low expectations and copying off the board;
- pupils in middle schools make more progress in Year 7 and Year 8 and less in Year 5 and Year 6 than similar pupils in a primary/secondary context;
- the authors conclude that the issue is transfer between schools, not transition between years;
- successful strategies include extended induction programmes, tracking, bridging units and intervention on managing learning;
- transfer is now less stressful but there is a lack of focus on teaching and learning.

The work we have been developing for some years at Ellowes Hall School attempted to address some or most of these issues well before this research was conducted. We are still on a journey of discovery and accept that we shall never reach a destination. The next section outlines some of the context, and work undertaken and still developing.

Learning to learn at Ellowes Hall School

The Ellowes Hall School is a mixed comprehensive school for the 11–19 age range set on the edge of the urban metropolitan borough of Dudley in the West Midlands. Our intake comes from families where a small minority (currently around 10 per cent) have experienced further or higher education opportunities. This figure has risen over the past ten years. Aspirations have been low traditionally. Twelve years ago our measure of success at GCSE was around 18 per cent of students obtaining five A*– C grades, and not expected to get much higher. Our free school meal percentage is, perhaps, surprisingly low (at around 13 per cent) and appears to be falling slowly. This masks the fact that a great majority of our intake come from families that lie just above this threshold economic measure. The intake is described as typically urban, 'white, working class', though some of the hard data might not suggest that this is so.

In recent years the intake has been in the lowest 5 per cent of attainment at Key Stage 2, though this is rising. Despite this we have achieved just over 40 per cent success at five A*– C, and should improve this figure in the future. Indeed, one of our targets is well over 50 per cent.

In 1990 it was announced that, as part of the local authority reorganisation, Ellowes Hall School would lose its sixth form and gain a Year 7 intake. The change from being a 12–18 school to 11–16 was not welcomed by the staff, or the parents. As far as the sixth form was concerned we had no choice (though this was a very strong feature in becoming a grant-maintained school three years later and reinstating our sixth form).

For Year 7, though, we had a choice. We could 'cry in our beer' and give the new Year 7s a Year 8 curriculum one year early, or do something else. We chose the latter option. Our discussions included a recognition that there was known to be a drop in performance on transfer to secondary school (this is not a new phenomenon, as we all know). The reasons for this were not well documented. At the same time, our broader agenda for improving the school also included a focus on teaching styles, and a desire to learn from best primary practice at the time.

It was our contention that children found it a traumatic experience to change from their comfort zone of 25 hours in one classroom, taught by one teacher who knew them 'inside out' and taught in a particular style, to flexibility in curriculum and time. These children were then faced with 30 lessons, 16 different rooms, 12 different teachers, hundreds of very large human beings, no classroom resources to hand, 12 different sets of expectations, bags and books to carry – all this and the dinners! Is it any wonder they did not make as much progress? It may be wondered that they made any progress at all (and indeed, for a while, some of them did not).

As a consequence, our ACT (Amalgamated Curriculum Time) programme was introduced nine years ago, originally aimed at addressing this drop in pupils' performance following transfer from primary to secondary school. There were three areas of focus that we identified in the challenges facing pupils on transfer to secondary schools – security, progression and continuity.

At this point it might be appropriate to review the original set of aims and objectives, written all those years ago. In what follows, nothing has been changed.

Amalgamated Curriculum Time in Year 7

The rationale

The perceptions that led to the development of the Year 7 strategy started many years ago. They were rooted in the belief that transfer to secondary school had been less effective and less efficient than it ought to have been. The major difficulties in transfer arrangements related to the issues of continuity, progression and security.

Continuity had been a problem in that children came from a number of primary schools into a completely new and alien environment. Transfer of records presented a challenge to schools which was not always addressed to the pupils' maximum benefit. Similarly, the induction process tended to be, as in many schools, no more than a brief tour of the school.

Progression was a principal concern because the assumption that we had to do it again to make sure they all had the basic skills' had been a common view held among secondary teachers. The confidence placed in primary colleagues was not as great as their dedication and skill warranted. Repetition meant inefficient use of time and, much worse, also resulted in diminishing the joy in learning through increasing frustration in pupils who regularly protested, 'We have already done this'. In addition, research has shown that staff expectations of pupils in secondary schools were often not as great as the pupils' capabilities warranted, and less had been expected of them than in their primary schools.

Lack of security was caused by the situation, for most children, of changing from a single teacher (based in one room) to as many as 15 different teachers (in as many locations). By its very nature this change (and other aspects associated with it) tended to be unsettling and, therefore, transition was less effective than it might have been.

The notion of a bridge curriculum (ACT 7) had resulted in better practices. However, the very nature of the word 'bridge' presupposed a joining, by an overarching structure, of two separate entities. This is not how we saw ACT 7. From its inception, ACT 7 looked more towards an educational highway on which pupils moved through the phase barrier without the need for slowing down or significant readjustment. ACT 7 aims to provide the security necessary for the smooth transition between primary and secondary school, as well as the curriculum continuity and progression to enable pupils to continue to enhance the joy of learning with which they are born.

Statement of intent

The intention of ACT is:

- to ensure a smooth transition of the development of skills, attitudes and knowledge between key stages, and between primary and secondary phases in particular;
- to ensure staff have a clear awareness and understanding of different teaching styles, different learning styles, and how to maximise their contributions across the whole curriculum;
- to provide a coherent set of curriculum experiences for each pupil;
- to help pupils understand the value of their educational experiences and their transferability between curriculum areas and into other contexts;
- to enhance the joy in learning with which we are born;
- to develop further the capacity of pupils for independent learning;
- to provide pupils with a rich diet of opportunities to develop a range of learning skills that will:
  - help them to learn how to learn more effectively;
  - serve them throughout their lives;
  - help enhance their intrinsic desire and motivation to learn;
- to provide substantial contact time with one teacher and, therefore, a secure learning base.

Desired outcomes

Building on their previous experiences, pupils will:

- feel secure about the transition between primary and secondary education through a clear and well-defined framework, providing continuity and progression in their learning;
- become well-integrated and independent people with self-esteem;
- respect other people;
- have their achievements recognised and rewarded.

Pupils will become independent learners through:

- experiencing a variety of teaching styles;
- developing a variety of learning skills that service the needs of the whole curriculum;
- being actively and responsibly involved in their learning;

- developing their positive attitude to learning;
- developing knowledge about subjects in the National Curriculum and other areas of the curriculum.

Parents will be involved whenever appropriate to provide support and guidance.

Links with primary schools will be strengthened.

A possible strategy for development

These brief notes outline a possible strategy for further development of the ACT 7 concept, and its contribution to the development of pupils as independent learners.

The curriculum might be based on such a framework, perhaps involving the following stages:

1 *Identification of learning skills*
   - from the existing programme (e.g. time management, research skills, library, project planning, etc.).
   - new skills (e.g. learning strategies, preferred learning styles, learning maps, etc.).

2 *Identification of contexts for skill development*
   - what National Curriculum areas/content will be covered?
   - what are the staff availability, capability and training needs?

3 *Devise assessment strategies*
   - to inform next steps in pupils' development;
   - to record progress in skill development;
   - to record progress through the National Curriculum;
   - to develop skills in self-assessment and review.

The skills developed in ACT will be transferable in order to service the rest of the curriculum, and will be reinforced there.

The response to the issue of security (which has echoes of Daniel Goleman's *Emotional Intelligence* (1995)) has been seen to be remarkably successful. To this end we introduced an amalgamated curriculum taught by one teacher per group for 30 per cent of curriculum time. The subjects in this scheme included the entire range bar modern foreign languages and physical education. A good primary practitioner was appointed to lead the team of volunteer staff and took up post two terms before the arrival of the first cohort of children. This preparation time was invaluable in developing attitudes and changing staff practices and approaches to teaching. The curriculum approaches adopted were those typical of best primary practice of the time and were based on a thematic approach to the curriculum.

At the same time we introduced Induction Week in July. All Year 6 pupils spent a week on 'normal' secondary timetable during which time we hoped they would accommodate many of the challenges facing them previously on transfer – changes of lesson and teacher, carrying belongings, for example. This has proved remarkably successful year on year.

Originally the ACT teachers were also the form tutors of these teaching groups, thus replicating to a significant extent the contact and security of the single-teacher relationship found in primary schools. At the same time the pupils developed confidence in coping with the hurly-burly of secondary school life with its large human beings, bells, movement between classrooms, carrying of bags, and coping with many different subjects and teachers. At the end of the first year, a Local Education Authority (LEA) evaluation indicated that the Year 7 pupils had made more progress and were further ahead than their Year 8 counterparts who had joined the school at the same time but without the benefit of this special programme.

However, the issues of progression and continuity were not addressed with the same measure of success. Indeed, the ACT programme had a number of false starts and setbacks. An Ofsted inspection in 1994 found it difficult to fit ACT into its framework, despite finding it making a very positive contribution to the pupils. The Ofsted view was to develop and embed the scheme, but the knee-jerk reaction that followed saw ACT time cut to 20 per cent of curriculum time, with the loss of several subjects. This has left a core of English, religious education (RE), personal, health and social education (PHSE) and information and communication technology (ICT) as the curriculum contexts.

Staffing problems followed. The original team leader left to return to the primary sector and the new appointee sadly became increasingly unwell, while ACT lost its centrality in the school and, in general, the school was perceived to be drifting. Illness resulted in two premature retirements, including the headteacher and the ACT team leader. A new team leader was appointed and, with another key change in personnel, ACT was 'reborn' and its purposes reaffirmed.

In 1999, the time was right for a new push to bring it all together and develop the good idea into a stunning reality. A new headteacher arrived and, inevitably, a number of changes took place. One of the most significant was the change to a mixed-age tutor system in order to help tutors monitor more closely and enhance the progress of every pupil. We had, as priority, that no pupil would be invisible and slip through the school without being noticed and their progress noted. The mixed-age tutor groups included four or five pupils from each year group (except for the sixth form who meet in their own sixth form centre).

These tutor groups of no more than 25 pupils allow the development of a 'family' ethos where older pupils enjoy the opportunity to support and care for their younger counterparts. The opportunities and encouragement for positive role models has transformed tutor time into a more civilised and focused period. Tutors' workload is spread across the year, thus allowing closer monitoring and support for every child in the school. One immediate consequence was that, typically, parents' consultation meetings had 95 per cent or higher attendance.

An Ofsted inspection in 1999, which judged the teaching and ethos very favourably, provided a basis for further improvement. The curriculum thrust was to move from a focus on teaching to one on learning. To this end we also started CASE in 1999, which has yet to see the first cohort through. A successful application was made in 2000 to become one of 24 pilot schools for a 'Learning to Learn' initiative organised by the Campaign for Learning. In this project we wished to develop a coherent programme of learning skills (including learning how to learn) across the curriculum, with special input in the ACT programme in Year 7. As part of the Dudley Grid for Learning (an authority-wide Public Funding Initiative/Public Private Partnerships project), in 2000 we installed a new ICT network of 150 computers in several bases throughout the school. This is a ten-year contracted, managed service and is a National Grid for Learning (NGFL) Pathfinder Project. All 62 teaching staff received their own laptops for curriculum and administration use. ICT is going to feature even more strongly to enhance learning in the future, but ACT is not a project about using ICT to enhance learning.

The ACT programme is currently being redesigned based on learning skills built into an amalgamated programme of English, RE, ICT and PHSE. A matrix of learning skills, styles and approaches has been drawn up, with the subjects providing the context for their exploration and application. For example, in the new programme pupils' preferred learning styles are identified and work schemes and lessons are designed to facilitate learners operating in different modes. Howard Gardner's concept of multiple intelligences (1983) is explored with pupils and their attributes are diagnosed. They are then helped to apply both of these theories in their approaches to their work, thus legitimising their differences and helping them to develop other ways of applying their natural strengths as learners. We hope that through these and other approaches, Guy Claxton's learnacy will become a reality in the curriculum experiences of our pupils.

We have certain ideas of particular interest that will feed back into the research dimension of the project. These include:

- the design of planned classroom interventions based on theories of learning styles and multiple intelligences in the four curriculum areas in ACT;
- the identification of pupils' preferred learning styles and predominant intelligences;
- the development of a staff booklet of learning approaches and techniques;
- the provision of a 'learning how to learn' induction course for pupils before arrival into the school at Year 7;
- the production of a 'learning how to learn' guide for parents.

Targets will be largely based on 'delivery' objectives (e.g. did it happen?) initially, and later on learning objectives (e.g. evidence of change of behaviour in learning situations). Evaluation will involve the collection and analysis of evidence from pupils and staff within the ACT programme and in other subject areas.

Validation of attitudinal and behavioural change in pupils will be necessary and will be carried out by survey and observation. A survey of pupils' attitudes to learning was conducted at the beginning of the year, with pupils from a similar school locally acting as the control group. This survey will be repeated at the end of the first year and the results analysed for similarities, differences and points of interest. In addition, an interim survey was carried out at the end of the first term with the Year 7 pupils at Ellowes Hall only. They were asked to respond to the questions by choosing a number from 1 to 4 to express their feelings, 4 being the highest. The 'control' question was D since Learning Maps were not introduced until the spring term! These results appear pleasing, as shown in Figure 2.1.

These responses are all the more pleasing given the staffing difficulties during this period. Our plans for a core team of 'emerging specialists' have been shaken by a long-term staff absence leading to ill-health retirement and other staff shortages resulting in four of the seven groups being taught by part-time supply teachers.

Staff attitude and practice surveys will be included to assess the extent to which staff change their professional practice. Other assessment data (e.g. Standard Assessment Tests (SATs) and school exams) will be included as appropriate. It will be important to moderate these data on the basis of prior attainment to eliminate variations between groups. It is hoped that the control group in the other school will continue to take part in the evaluation process.

Other data contributing to the evaluation might include internally moderated and standardised subject test data to assess the transferability of such approaches into other subjects where the approaches are not being 'taught'. Comparisons with 'hard' data from previous years may be used, though we recognise the potential for the invalidity of comparisons between different cohorts. Data on misbehaviour and attendance patterns during the year may also be analysed. Videos of teaching, peer observation and learning diaries will be incorporated where possible.

Phase 2 will involve spreading the understanding and application of this work throughout all subject areas in Year 7, into all other year groups, and subsequently to parents. Staff training for the ACT team takes place regularly and is planned for all staff in order to develop their knowledge and share the good practice already identified. Reinforcement of these experiences and new approaches will be embedded later in the school life of each pupil. While these core activities and developments will continue to take place in ACT in Year 7, ultimately it is our aim that all curriculum experiences will be based on these theories and approaches to learning.

LEARNING TO LEARN PUPIL SURVEY   Dec. 2000

What have you learned about yourself as a learner this term?

		GIRLS					BOYS			
		1	2	3	4		1	2	3	4
A	I have a more positive attitude towards learning	0%	12%	75%	12%		2%	15%	70%	13%
B	I am better at planning my work	0%	23%	56%	21%		3%	26%	49%	21%
C	I co-operate well when I work	0%	5%	56%	39%		3%	8%	59%	30%
D	I can use Learning Maps to help me	73%	6%	12%	9%		79%	5%	13%	3%
E	I can set myself targets which I can achieve if I work well	1%	19%	53%	26%		8%	11%	47%	34%
F	I know the conditions in which I work best	0%	10%	42%	48%		6%	10%	53%	38%

How do you feel as a learner this term?

		GIRLS					BOYS			
		1	2	3	4		1	2	3	4
G	I am feeling more confident as a learner	1%	9%	47%	43%		3%	9%	44%	44%
H	I know what to do when I get stuck	0%	5%	30%	65%		3%	5%	36%	55%
I	I feel good about myself as a learner	0%	14%	68%	18%		6%	17%	54%	23%
J	The words that describe me best as a learner are:	1%	4%	34%	61%		1%	5%	26%	68%

1. *I can't do things well*
2. *I don't know what to choose*
3. *I can do things well*
4. *I can do some things and others I can't do yet*

Figure 2.1 The Ellowes Hall School 'learning to learn' pupil survey

How will this make a difference? Clearly, any response to this question is speculative, but we would hope to see a number of things, including:

- improvement in learning skills;
- increased confidence;
- increased motivation to learn;
- increased autonomy for learners;
- increased engagement in learning (including beyond school days);
- improvement in examination success for pupils at all levels of attainment;
- better employment prospects;
- decreased disaffection and disruption among pupils;
- greater job satisfaction for teachers.

If we achieve this, we will be delighted.

And finally ...

It is my contention that teachers hold the future of Britain in their hands, both in terms of our society and our economy. Opportunities for formal and informal learning at all ages will be vital to equip people to turn information into knowledge and to apply wisdom to that knowledge, thus enabling people to make the most of their talents and opportunities.

Sadly, 10 per cent of the 16–24-year-old age group (well over half a million young people) are not in work, full-time education or training, or claiming unemployment-related benefit. They have effectively dropped out of the official statistics completely. The great majority underachieved at school and many played truant. Most if not all are part of that tragic and unavoidable underclass of those who cannot, or will not, engage in learning.

Low self-esteem and lack of self-belief, uncertainty and risk have prevented learning taking place. We must strive to engage these youngsters in learning and help them develop the confidence and positive attitudes of mind to maintain their engagement. The other 90 per cent of us will benefit also.

References

Black, P. and Wiliam, D. (1998) 'Assessment and classroom learning' in *Assessment in Education: Principles, policy and practice.* London: King's College.

Claxton, G. (2000) 'Learning to learn' conference. London: Campaign for Learning.

Galton, M., Gray, J. and Ruddock, J. (1999) *The Impact of School Transitions and Transfers on Pupil Progress and Attainment.* London: DfEE.

Gardner, H. (1983) *Frames of Mind: The theory of multiple intelligences.* New York: Basic Books.

Gilbert, I. (2000) 'Qualified for what?' in *Headlines* (journal of the Secondary Heads Association).

Goleman, D. (1995) *Emotional Intelligence: Why it can matter more than IQ.* New York: Bantam Books.

Honey, P. (1999) www.peterhoney.com/declaration (version 1).

Maclean, P. (1983) *The Triune Brain.* New York: Plenum.

Sperry, R. (1974) 'Lateral specialization in the surgically separated hemispheres' in Schmitt, F. and Worden, F. (eds) *Neurosciences Third Study Program*, 3: 5–19. Cambridge: MIT Press.

West-Burnham, J. (2000) 'The school of the future' in *Headlines* (journal of the Secondary Heads Association), Issue 31.

Zohar, D. and Marshall, I. (2000) *SQ: Connecting With Our Spiritual Intelligence.* London: Bloomsbury.

3

■ ■ ■

Standards are for Life,
Not Just the League Tables

by Mike Hardacre

Context

I became a head in 1988 just as the teacher union disputes which had characterised the early to mid-1980s had finally been put to bed by Baker's imposition of the 1265 hours. It saw the introduction of Local Management of Schools (LMS) at a time when the government was rolling out its National Curriculum reforms; the grant-maintained sector; and the spurious concept of open enrolment. It was an era that moved power to central government by emasculating local government's tax-raising capabilities and led to the destabilisation of local democratic control systems to the extent that we now see the government seriously questioning the viability of local education authorities. It has also brought, conversely, the attempt to fill the power vacuum by bolstering the position of the governing body. The thrust of these two drives has led directly to a situation where residual local authorities can be almost totally disempowered while schools appear to have been set free subject only to the power of the Department for Education and Employment and the Learning and Skills Councils (LSCs).

The particular school context in which I took up headship was not atypical. It was an inner-urban school of 600 pupils, with 170 leaving and 99 coming in, a diminutive sixth form and a decline in numbers that was steeper than demography suggested it should be. The school served what was perceived to be a tough, white, working-class, 1960s overspill council estate. The nearest school was the grammar school that had been renamed a comprehensive while still behaving as if it was the grammar school. The authority published a multi-option closure plan in my first year, in which the school was named for closure in 12 out of 13 options. There was a degree of internal malaise about the school – no enforcement of school rules, a five-minute morning staff briefing which was always on the edge of being turned into a debating society, and a staff that saw a split between management (head and senior management team (SMT) known as 'the hierarchy') and the rest of the staff. This meant that the school lacked a policy direction and had led to an air of tired crisis management. It would not be difficult to provide further examples of a school drifting away from the SMT and governors and into potential oblivion.

The area was recovering from the destruction of the manufacturing base in iron and steel in the West Midlands, unemployment was high, qualifications among parents were low, distrust and disbelief that any of the institutions could actually help was high, casual employment was the order of the day. There were a large number of unemployed fathers whose real existence had been defined by their employment.

There were, however, many good things that the school had going for it and it was from those that I had to advance the school. At the core was a committed group of parents who wanted their children to do well. I was fortunate enough to inherit a strong and thoughtful SMT who were all prepared to roll up their sleeves and change the internal expectations and external perceptions of the school. There was a strong tradition of an annual musical which was the centrepiece of parental and community involvement with the school. *Carousel*, *The Sound of Music* and *Oklahoma* were better known on the estate than some of the musical events that the school now puts on. The deputy who produced them had a real feel for the cultural mores of our parents and even then at least a quarter to a third of the school was involved in the production. The school had a tradition of high-quality individual pastoral care but a tradition that lacked a policy direction. The art and mathematics departments had high-quality teaching and achievement, but the rest of the school was a real 'curate's egg', about which there was no coherence of policy or direction. Nor was there any acknowledgement of the need to 'play for the school team'.

Moving on

I have always had a soft spot for the description by the 16th-century Holy Roman Emperor, Charles V, of his task of trying to control Spain, Italy, Germany, the Netherlands and the papacy: 'It was like trying to compress a huge mattress – where he was there might be control, but everywhere else troubles rose around him.' Although neither holy, Roman nor an emperor, I felt as if I had some empathy with Charles.

Having painted a picture of where the school was, I hope in the remainder of this chapter to show how the school moved from its potential closure, its disarray and its malaise, to become a 900-strong, successful working-class comprehensive without concentrating its efforts upon a repressive, inhibiting, academic standards-led agenda. I believe that the creation of the appearance of change is essentially a short-term fix and that the reality of change with substance is a long-haul operation. The changes I will write about did not happen all at once but grew organically over a period of 12 years.

I resolved to ensure that those policies that the school had should be implemented. This included insisting that Year 10 and 11 boys should wear blazers, otherwise there was no point in having a uniform policy. Nothing brings a school into greater disrepute than not meaning what you say; indeed, it renders it more difficult to operate any other school policy.

I am a great believer in capitalising upon those things that people hold to be in the best interest of the school. My view was that the school needed to heighten its profile. It needed also to adopt a much more structured approach to publicise the good practice that was taking place in patches throughout the school, 'accentuating the positive and eliminating the negative'. Restructuring of timetables and staffing was put through in the first year. This coincided with the ability to use the authority's local management scheme to start doing the things that staff felt had been ignored – refurbishment, redecoration and the like. School rules were to be enforced, staff were to be backed up, parents were to be reminded that the school was about the education of their children, not about sorting out the perennial family disagreements that were forever being brought into the school. The option system was dismantled in order to install the National Curriculum. Children were not allowed to drop a language at the end of Year 9 and we went for a straightforward delivery of the National Curriculum. This meant that some of those areas that were successful were actually diminished and that the pre-eminence which some departments had appeared to have was curtailed. The school had been run a little bit along the lines of a convoy in which one did not proceed at a uniform pace but in which resources were given to those who were prepared to talk up their own departmental contribution.

The school needed to be welded together and that was my first aim.

Corporate strategy

No school can move forward without the subscription of the staff to a common and corporate view of what the school is for and what it is trying to achieve. It is vitally important in these circumstances that the team in general and the head in particular sets a climate whereby people can be allowed to develop their professional and classroom expertise within a framework that is not about blaming but about setting minimum standards to which all should sub-scribe. Given a newly appointed head's inheritance of strong characters, this is not always an easy task. If there is no clarity from the head, there can be no clarity for classroom teachers or for any of the layers in between the head and classroom teachers. The greatest assistance that can be given to staff, in my opinion, is clear, short and concise job descriptions that enable them to under-stand their part in both communication and ensuring that progress can be made. These days, this sort of approach is often target-led against external standards. It need not be. The needs for staff can be very simply expressed as 'any teaching or administrative arrangements they make that fall below the standards of care they would expect for their own children are not good enough for other people's children'.

There must be massive encouragement by the team to ensure that this process is positive rather than carpingly negative. There is a place for the negative, but it is not in public. The climate that must be created is one where the school is moving forward and upwards from wherever it is at the time that you examine it. This requires great resilience and willingness on the part of senior, middle and lower management levels. Staff must be encouraged to set the highest stan-dards possible for children. It is the job of the team to assist them in the enforcing of rules and standards. Lest one thinks that this means the homogeni-sation of staff and the curtailing of individuality, it is not so. It actually means that all individuals must be encouraged to take their own perceptions within a very clear framework of improvement and good professional relationships with others. This is the bedrock of a school. No school can allow individual egos to overcome the expressed ethos that the governors and senior team seek for their school. It puts great emphasis upon the senior team's ability to spot and identify what needs to be done for the children of their community.

Improvement for children should be seen as building upon individuals' com-petences and abilities. There cannot necessarily be a year-on-year rise in achievement. Raw scores and league tables are a scandalous misuse of data, for they take no regard of quality of intake, nor do they give any credence to the 'value added' concept. It is clearly grossly unfair to judge a school with 25 per cent free school meals entitlement against a school with less than 5 per cent free school meals entitlement. Senior teams cannot afford to let external pressures overcome the need to deal with their individual community.

However, it is also clear that regard has to be taken of what children should be able to achieve and to ensure that staff push children towards maximum per-formance concomitant with good psychological health. If that is true of children, it is equally true of staff. I do not and cannot approve of ways of deal-ing with staff that actually push them to the edge of breakdown – that is a recipe for greater disaster. The staff are the most precious commodity that the head has in ensuring the health and wellbeing of the school. This has to mean that within a collective framework due regard must be given to individual needs not only for children but also for staff. I have long held a vision that schools are places where children can make mistakes in safety and learn from them. Holding that view for children has made it rather easier to deal with staff when they too have found themselves in a position where they have not always thought through the consequences of their individual action. The staff need to be moved together collectively. It is important for heads and senior staff to remember that those who make the greatest noise may be the only people making a noise about the issue and may not be representative of the whole staff.

All syllabuses and schemes of work were to be written up to a substantially common framework that was then placed in every lending library in our catchment area so that parents could refer to the work that children should be doing. This move towards a 'publicity'-driven view of the school was part of a thrust that was not written but carried in my head. I resolved every week to write at least two positive press releases about children's successes. Although my colleague heads came to the assumption that I had a majority share in all the local newspaper and television companies, the spin-off was the feeling of self-worth that was engendered for children and parents. After all, it was their school (rather than the local selective, by ability or class, school) that was appearing in the paper. The high spot of this approach was when our local free paper carried a quarter-page spread on a group of 30 Year 7 children who had visited our local library, under the headline '*Students Read Books*'! The low spot was being beheaded 15 times for Midlands television as the culmination of a multi-departmental French activities day in which several staff and I had spent the morning recreating the French Revolution. And yes, the languages department did teach everybody the words and meaning of the *Marseillaise*, the music department got them to sing it, the drama teacher and I directed it and the craft design technology department built the guillotine. I spent 15 anxious times with my head on the block – not dissimilar to a normal morning in headship!

Community and communication

Community involvement in the school had tended to be through a small but vociferous Parent Teacher Association, a local tenants' group who would have preferred houses to have been built on the school site 22 years earlier, and the community choir which had been created by the hard work of one of the deputies. The reality was that most of these groups were the same people, but the danger was that they were an unrepresentative clique who could influence the school to ensure it was run round their children. With support from my senior team, I decided that if there was a learning issue for staff and pupils, there was also a learning and confidence issue for the community. I performed the traditional visitations of the new head round the feeder primary schools and resolved to keep my mouth shut and listen carefully to my primary colleagues' perceptions of the school. This was not an easy task, but it behoves us not to be too bombastic about how we manage secondary education, as many of our primary colleagues feel themselves to be, and actually are, the poor relations.

Through the combined information that came from all these sources it was clear that the catchment area had something of a crisis of confidence in the school. There was a perception of bullying and a rough, tough environment which, when coupled with the slightly run-down air caused by a maintenance backlog, produced an antipathy to the school and a belief that children did not have a quality learning environment. During the first few months I looked at my catchment area and tried to position the school uniquely. It was clear with our academic record that the school was not in a position to compete with the six academically selective schools within an 8 kilometre radius. Nor was it in a position to compete academically with the three church schools all less then 6.5 kilometres away, whose intake was skewed towards the aspirant and the successful.

We decided as a senior team that the internal behaviour patterns of the school had to be changed. The senior team were everywhere in the school rooting out disruptive behaviour in the classroom. I took a high profile in dealing with behaviour in the community outside school time by invoking the 'bringing the school into disrepute' card permanently to exclude a small but very significant group of Year 11 students. Careful use was also made of fixed-term exclusion to deal with breaches of classroom behaviour. It is important to remember in this area that parents are naturally angry and insecure and need treating with courtesy, clarity and firmness. It is time-consuming to deal with parents who are suspicious and disbelieving, but it is worth every difficult minute spent in rational explanation. Some of the most 'difficult' parents became some of the school's best supporters. Some, of course, still harboured resentments, but this became a decreasing minority.

These approaches brought immediate gains as parents began to believe in our ability to ensure a proper learning environment for children. It also led to the area ceasing to be a juvenile crime hotspot and becoming a reasonably peaceful, law-abiding area. This did not diminish the skill and expertise needed by staff to perform in the classroom, but it provided a base from which they could work on the attainment of children as well as improving their behaviour.

While it is important to make the mattress even and get rid of the lumps, it is also vital to keep innovation alive and to encourage and maintain out-of-classroom activities. These are the real lifeblood of the school. We went for three weeks, instead of one, to the authority's outdoor pursuits centre: once for a biology field trip, once for a geography field trip and once for the traditional outdoor pursuits trip. Attendance on the courses was based on school attendance, behaviour and aptitude displayed over the calendar year prior to the trip. Just as children need to be rewarded for getting matters right, so too do the teaching staff. The decision to subsidise these trips placed a financial burden on the school budget but it was clear to me that the returns in behaviour and esteem they created made it worth depriving departments of extra glue sticks.

One of the most valuable projects for a school is to be involved in a Comenius project which is designed to enhance international curriculum and teacher exchange. Ours was between vocational schools in Italy, Hungary, Sweden and the Czech Republic. Students took part in exchange visits with Sweden and Hungary. We took the school choir and band to Hungary. This was the first time abroad for many of our students. The choir and orchestra joined with our Hungarian partners to play to a packed town hall in Budapest, an amazing and deeply emotional experience for all of us, including for the child who decided to ring her parents on her mobile at 11.45 pm on the Saturday we arrived. The parents then rang us to say that she was homesick and feeling unwell. Cue for a trip in a Hungarian taxi by two staff to the home where the student was, to find by the time they arrived that everything was fine and problems were settled. All part of life's rich tapestry!

Communications with parents and the community offer some easy but decisive victories in changing people's perceptions of the school. I recommend changing the layout and colour of the school notepaper, always writing in 14-point type, putting on the paper any relevant logos. By the time I left, the notepaper had gone through several transformations but had at that time the Schools Curriculum Award, Investors in People and two Charter Marks (given by the Cabinet Office in recognition of outstandingly high quality public service). Remember, too, you are an exam centre for a variety of boards who also have logos. Always try to write with a layperson's vocabulary, always proof a letter several times and as a final check get someone who has never seen it to read it. Be prepared to scrap letters, newsletters and the like – even if you have 1000 of them printed – if they contain a grammar or spelling mistake. Nothing makes schools look more ridiculous than bad spelling or grammar in letters to the public. I always insisted that all communications went through the head before they were sent out and if staff had made spelling errors, sent it back to them for correction. It may be time-consuming but in the end it will be quicker as your need to proof will diminish.

The staff

My next comments may seem facile in the context of a teacher recruitment crisis, but there is no substitute for appointing staff who personify the beliefs of the school. If the details you send to candidates are crystal clear about the belief structure of the school and show how that works out in practice, you will receive applications only from those committed to the school's philosophy. There is also no excuse for failing to develop the staff you have. It is important to have the minimum of meetings necessary to conduct business. A meeting will not *per se* improve the quality of classroom delivery, nor will it ensure a sports team arrives at its destination, ensure a rehearsal of the brass group, or let the librarian run a homework club. If the philosophy of the school is expressed with absolute clarity and the pragmatic workings are clear, then meetings should be few, succinct and purposeful. It is, indeed, in the non-classroom events that the health of the school is shown. A meeting pattern that takes up all the hours that Baker gave is one that will totally destroy the life of the school. This means that the senior team has to be proactive about turning the staff towards task completion rather than time fulfilment. The senior team will need to be selective about which tasks the school should be pursuing. The school cannot do everything it is asked to do and the classroom staff need protecting from overload. Would that the same could be said for senior management.

It is hard to remember that a minor miracle occurs in every secondary school in the country every day. Some 800 hormonally active students come into the school and are taught by 55 staff for eight lessons a day plus two pastoral sessions. Assuming that each member of staff interacts once per lesson with each student, I make that 440 000 human interactions, not including anything that passes off between students. Given that scale of interaction it is a miracle that schools are such well maintained and ordered communities. This can be achieved only by ensuring that the school is a listening community that values all its members, whether staff, pupils, parents or community. It is important to remember that it is the hope of reward that sweetens labour, so every opportunity should be taken to offer extrinsic reward. It is a small minority, impelled by sense of duty or whatever, who work only for intrinsic satisfaction. Create and find every opportunity to tell your whole community what a good job they are doing.

One of the most unlikely places to find opportunities to make people feel valued is the exclusion process. This is an area fraught with difficulty and anxiety for those concerned. The various forums in which events have to take place are both a difficulty and an advantage. The procedures have the facility to depersonalise and de-emotionalise the decision-making process but it is the job of the skilled professional to ensure that no matter how heinous the crime, all participants retain their self-esteem. As head you have to accept that you may not 'win' all hearings and it is important in that context that as the skilled professional it is for the head to massage frayed sensibilities so that re-entry is as painless and smooth as possible.

I can recommend highly the employment of a school counsellor to mediate the re-entry programme. It became a condition of re-entry that every excluded student, no matter how short the exclusion, had to have one meeting with the school counsellor and then was given the option of whether or not they wished to continue with the meetings. The vast majority of students did continue for a period of time and many told me how valuable they found it in giving them the tools for anger management.

To sum up

What I have written so far is a kaleidoscopic impression of some of the many developments that made, I believe, the school of which I was head for 13 years a good school. If I were to summarise, the points would be:

- clearly articulated vision;
- clear working out of that vision at a pragmatic operational level;
- identifying the school with parental aspirations for their children;
- close involvement with all the community;
- involving parents, pupils, staff and community in the learning process;
- a learning environment infusing all aspects of school life;
- never offering what you know you cannot deliver;
- the public face of the school is well served by high quality performing arts;
- schools must be managed and lead pro-actively;
- there is no substitute for quality staff and (sometimes) their idiosyncrasies;
- there is no substitute for writing documents in plain English without jargon;
- no individual ego can be allowed to be bigger than the school;
- counselling makes a difference;
- say what you do and do what you say.

The last of these is particularly important as the whole edifice will collapse if there is not synchronicity between public statements and a school's dealings with all its community.

4

■ ■ ■

Staying Alive: The Price of School Improvement

by Irene Dalton and John Read

The curse of Wombwell High School is that it has been, in recent history, always just slightly ahead of the national agenda. The second is that 'funny money' always arrives about a year after we need it.

Wombwell High School is an 11–16 comprehensive school of 850 pupils and 44 teaching staff, serving three former pit villages on the outskirts of Barnsley, South Yorkshire. The area is just beginning to pick up after the traumas of the miners' strike of 1984 but is still one of high unemployment, with 29 per cent of pupils having an entitlement to free school meals. The school has declined in numbers since 1987, mainly for demographic reasons, from 1150 to 859 pupils and the teaching staff from 74 (1987) to 44 (2001), a ratio of 26 per cent pupil number reduction to a 40 per cent reduction in staff.

When the current head, Irene Dalton, arrived in 1987, the school presented a picture of total neglect. A skip stood opposite the school entrance in what had been a shrubbery, a pile of broken desks and milk crates littered the foyer, windows were filthy, and she discovered, on opening the lid of the grand piano, two empty coke cans. The classroom furniture was, frankly, a disgrace: circa 1950, with years of carefully worked graffiti and most of the desk lids off their hinges. Irene's first act was to throw out (physically) all the furniture in the head's study, including the head's chair (typist's version, with designer stuffing hanging out) and the net curtains (stained with smoke and holes neatly held together by long sewing needles). She then worked on the floor for two months until the chief education officer (CEO) made other arrangements.

Pupils were placed in top, middle and bottom bands, and although the school had its share of caring and committed staff, the description 'a band X' pupil was common currency. Also common currency were low expectations of behaviour. Some aggressive pupils went relatively unchallenged and while the small sixth form was successful, expectations beyond this academic group were low, with General Certificate of Secondary Education (GCSE) results bobbing between 14 and 16 per cent. Some people seemed to care about the academic pupils, some about those with special needs, but nobody seemed to care for the whole group of children. Certainly there was no sense of equal value. The senior management team had traditional roles, curriculum (which in those days meant timetable) and and pastoral deputies, and heads of sixth, upper and lower school. They did not, however, operate as a team – they got on with their individual jobs and referred to the head when a big decision had to be made.

This is the story of how a change in culture, ethos and values has made a difference: a change brought about by people, not money, by love and some passion, not force-feeding.

Adversity

Certain changes were made early. The three-band system was ended and in 1988, before the National Curriculum arrived, a 100 per cent core curriculum was brought in. In addition, most subjects changed from a streamed to a mixed-ability delivery.

In 1988, the new head introduced departmental 'visits'– mini formal inspections – with strong support and advice from the district HMI and some disquiet from Local Education Authority (LEA) advisers. These were of value principally because the head had the opportunity, then very rare, to observe many lessons over a short period in a single department, to experience the conditions in which the teaching took place, and to have extended interviews with all members of the department. For the first time they discussed what they felt about their situation and how they saw their role in the way the department functioned.

Some minor but significant changes were made as a result. The modern languages department was re-sited on the top floor of a three-storey block and carpeted, thus eliminating the problems it had had on the ground floor when, in large echoing rooms with a lot of pupils passing for, say, vaccinations, it had been impossible to concentrate on listening skills. A technician was redeployed from science to the arts department when the sixth form was closed in 1989 because during a 'visit' a very able music teacher had to spend his whole break packing up and securing electronic keyboards before the next class came in.

There had been tiny improvements in results when, within six weeks in the winter of 1990–1991, we had two serious fires, one destroying the craft, design and technology block, and the other the whole administration block, staff room, the hall and 19 classrooms. Nobody who has not shared the experience of such devastation can imagine what it feels like. Nor can they imagine the period of the rebuild when the cold in the unheated, unused sections of the school seeps into your very bones. The architects used the phrase 'a dead building' and that was an exact description.

The rebuild took two years, partly to replace what we had lost but also because the architects on site found that the rest of the buildings, a legacy of the 1960s, were unfit for the purpose – something we had been telling the LEA for ages. Rain was coming in so that children had to sit 1.5 metres from the windows. A gap of 15 centimetres opened up on the third floor between floor and wall whenever a high wind blew. Power points had to be isolated in the laboratories because they were permanently wet when it rained. Two full three-storey blocks ended up having to be re-clad from the outside. We were a building site for more than two years.

Naturally, while the school was in this state, external vandalism increased, self-esteem dropped, we lost numbers, and when the buildings were complete in summer 1992, we faced our worst ever examination results: 12 per cent A*–Cs. Our attendance rate was in the low 80s and we were surrounded by a sea of trampled mud. Many able children were opting for other schools. All we had was the spirit with which we had carried on during the rebuild, beautiful new buildings and some marvellous children. Oh yes, we also had the security fence; the insurers had insisted that the LEA provided one.

Without doubt, before such a phrase had ever been heard, we were a failing school. (Wombwell was well in advance of the national agenda in this too.)

One of the head's favourite stories is from her first week, when a panting Year 9 boy had almost dragged her from her study to the back gate, shouting: 'There's a dust cart pouring muck into our playground!'. After a mutual exchange of views, the dustcart left. Head and boy returned, with him saying: 'Well done, Miss, it may be a dump, but it's ours!'.

And in that incident, and the staff of Wombwell's capacity to react to the honesty and worth of its pupils, lies the seed of the changes that we brought about.

Sowing the seeds of change

They began in 1993, when Sue Fenna, head of physical education (PE) and a keen gardener, asked for £200 from the budget for plants to make the place look better. She had a vision, 'Operation Campus', which would transform the school environment. Sue and the head agreed that they would get it going over a half term, Sue being determined that when the staff came back they would see a real difference. With two people hired from parks and gardens, and a Rotavator, the two mad women of Wombwell slogged for a full day, from nine in the morning to five at night, filling beds with shrubs; they erected tiny fences to make a barrier till the shrubs grew; finally, still upright but struggling, they hammered in metal posts and strung up orange tape to signal 'keep off the borders'.

The effect was amazing. Sue rapidly recruited the 'Campus Team', a group of about 20 pupils prepared to turn out every Friday after school and on some Saturday mornings to dig, hoe, weed and plant. Because the children created the gardens, every child had a personal stake in the way the place looked: no damage was done; no one walked on the grass; litter was a rarity. Sue cadged top soil from here, garden benches from there, heavy machinery to dig up tarmac from somewhere else. She found us six business partners who gave £250 a year to support the improvements. The Campus Team won competitions, such as the best regional school in the Britain in Bloom competition in 1996 (previous winners had tended to be junior schools in pretty villages). They were rewarded by meeting botanist David Bellamy, and won a national competition which supplied the cost of half an outdoor classroom. The school became a beautiful environment. More important, the children noticed the difference, and began to comment adversely on schools they visited for sports matches. As they realised that their school was 'the best' in this aspect, they began to believe that they were the best, too. The head kept plugging away in assemblies, as heads do, that yes, we were the greatest, we would be the best school in the land. (Though the results were still nothing to write home about; indeed, the less said, the better.)

At roughly the same time, a new deputy head was appointed. David Jackson was the first to use the term, now precious to us, 'The Achievement Culture'. By this we meant creating a culture where to succeed was the norm, to mess about or fail to achieve was exceptional. He instituted our awards evenings, with a system of commendations leading to a major presentation evening, very formal in the hall, with parents and honoured guests, speeches, applause and tea and buns. It still goes on, but now we have to have separate evenings for upper and lower school for, although we have not changed the criteria for awards, the numbers of pupils gaining one has doubled. The proportion of boys to girls receiving awards has also greatly increased. David also had a gift for making people – staff and pupils – feel good, something much needed at the time. Again, we were ahead of the national agenda: good competitive sport; a good teaching environment; rewarding pupils; community and business involvement; some 'traditional values'.

No quick fixes

In 1994, with league tables firmly established, we realised that more had to be done. Self-esteem was high, the place felt good, but we knew that our results and attendance were not good enough and would not stand the scrutiny of the new Ofsted regime. Whatever was to be done, the senior management team were committed to building to last – quick fixes were not an option. The strategic direction of the school was decided upon. First, we tackled self-esteem, based on pride in the community and environment (we had got that far), then good behaviour and uniform, then a broad spectrum of success for all: on which base we would hope steadily to erect the future of high academic attainment (and a good place in the league tables). We also took a decision not to bid for any funding unless it fitted into our strategy and we could sustain any grant-funded developments out of budget should the money dry up. (We had seen others caught that way before.)

Those who talk about the importance of visionary leadership and then of strategic planning, as if the one were thrilling and the other mechanical, miss the point. Vision comes first. You have to be able to see the 'sunny dome and the towers of ice'. But if you are going to get there you need a strategy, and that is good, solid, intellectual endeavour. Neither vision nor strategy get you far, however, without the leadership that interprets vision and strategy into implementation through the sheer hard work and attention to detail that is good management. The strength of our current leadership group is that between us we share the main components of an 'ideal' team: we have a 'plant', a 'shaper', an implementer, a 'chairman', a 'company worker' and a 'finisher'. We are bound by our commitment to the school, a strong sense of humour, and genuine care for each other.

We had the environment and self-esteem. The next step in the strategy was an ethos of good behaviour. We knew we needed a behaviour policy based on what is now called positive behaviour management, but we also knew that this, if it were to be effective, would have to be hammered out by proper, probably lengthy, consultation with all parties. John Read had been in the school since 1982, first as head of PE, then as assistant head of the lower school. In 1994 he became assistant head of pastoral care. Since 1998 he has been deputy head (pupil management) and that title is significant.

John took the lead in the biggest 'purge' the school has ever known, tackling attendance and behaviour at the same time. At that point we had 82 per cent attendance and, for Year 11, 53 per cent for part of the year. We commissioned a report on our attendance procedures from David Bottomley, one of the LEA educational psychologists. He said our procedures were not co-ordinated and there were gaps in communication, making them not fully effective. John's first step was to take a strong line on attendance, insisting on notes, not authorising any doubtful absence, checking figures weekly, giving a prize for the top form in every year each week, closing the register very early so that our hard core lates became absent, and instituting detentions with year tutors for lates. In short, he made attendance a big issue for pupils, staff and, above all, for parents. Attendance figures plummeted further. But then they began to increase – we were making such a fuss that it was hard for pupils and parents to carry on being away from school on thin pretexts.

Ahead of the time

By the time of the Ofsted inspection in November 1994, attendance was just over 90 per cent. The work involved was, and still is, phenomenal. Again, we were ahead of the time. An irony (there will be others) is that by 2000, attendance stood at the national average, with unauthorised absence at 0.6 per cent. Then along came the Pupil Retention Grant. We were told to reduce unauthorised absence, and the LEA set us a target of reducing by a consistent 0.03 per cent (no, that is not a misprint!) per term over the year of the grant. All that we had previously achieved in this area – without any additional help or funding – was ignored: we still had to reduce the figures. (Actually, so far we have: we like to win.) The Pupil Retention Grant provided the things we had needed for so long, including clerical assistance for first day call. We had already tried this, the head and deputy doing it themselves for a trial period of six weeks. It worked well, but we could not afford the time to keep it going.

The second thrust John made was on behaviour, and with that, uniform. He created a vast chart (with a PE and geography background, what else?) on his wall, with every pupil's name on it and a grid. Anyone unwise enough to arrive without a tie, sport a wrong jumper, deck themselves in jewellery, flaunt their designer trainers or forget equipment was summoned, warned and recorded on the chart. Even the wearing of shirts not firmly tucked into trousers was forbidden. After three warnings came a detention. Resistance petered out fairly rapidly. A deputy head who never forgets – and can produce the evidence – is very hard to resist. Form tutors were active in checking uniform. Senior managers let their eyes run over uniform with elaborate interest in assembly. The standard of dress became very high and the difference in the way the pupils looked began to match the environment. We genuinely believe they felt better for it, too. One of the advantages of school uniform, properly worn, is its formality. Many current modes of dress have disturbingly aggressive overtones. Formal dress implies that you are in a place of business, a place where people work. It is not about control; it is about dignity and presenting a corporate ethos. Staff dress codes are equally important, and convey messages which pupils are quick to interpret, mainly in the way they do or do not challenge teachers.

Unacceptable behaviour was defined and we used the term 'zero tolerance', just ahead of Tony Blair's pre-election pronouncements. We believed that if minor misconduct was ignored, then serious poor behaviour would be much more difficult to deal with. We instituted 'walk on the left', 'walk one abreast' rules, and paid attention to flow of movement on stairs and to the dining hall for dinners. The environment helped us – by now pupils had plenty of seats outside during social times, and outdoor basketball courts to run off energy. All this quietened down pupil movement, particularly at lunchtime. Nobody reported for misbehaviour to senior staff escaped the net. The duty officers, senior staff on call throughout teaching time, were run ragged. Every incident was logged in John Read's black book, where each week he transcribed (and still does) against every pupil's name a record of every commendation, every detention, every duty officer call-out and every 'incident sheet' (our record of events worth bringing to the attention of year tutors, short of asking for immediate help). The head believes this chapter might have been entitled 'One Man and his Log'.

The key was staying on top of things, feeling the pulse of the school, knowing what was going on. If John ever said, 'We need to get out there today', no one questioned it. Similarly, if any member of staff, including the head, ever marched into his office saying that 10X were getting out of hand, he would calmly reach for the log, run his finger down the relevant page and tell them exactly who was not behaving well, who had recently improved, and who was not, and never had been, guilty of anything. We also used our two days a week (now cut to one) Barnsley Education Service Support Team (BEST) member, a trained counsellor, to work with pupils proactively. She worked on bullying, anger management, outreach work with parents and improving self-esteem, in ways from losing weight to having the confidence to entertain senior staff for coffee, homemade cakes and a chat. Leaders of the school council, a slowly maturing body (we will get to democracy, as Bernard Trafford describes it in his chapter, one day), conducted a bullying survey, analysed the results and presented them to the full staff at a formal meeting. This took some courage on both sides.

This log underpins the basis of a particular trust by pupils. They know that no accusation will stick unless there is real evidence, unless the incident has been thoroughly investigated, unless the senior staff are satisfied that they have got as close to the truth as is possible. Again, this is time consuming, and it should be known that at this point in the school's life, the pupil:teacher ratio had risen to 21:6. Exclusions rocketed during this period, but they declined rapidly in 1994–1995.

Strategy of success

In the summer of 1994 our examination results were 27 per cent A*–C grades, a rise from 14 per cent in the previous year. When Ofsted came, the praise for the school's behaviour management was glowing. We had done very little directly to improve results, beyond some gestures towards trying to make some D grades into Cs. It was the improvement in ethos, behaviour and attitude to school, talking up the achievement culture, and the sense of purpose that the atmosphere conveyed, that made the difference. This was no accident, nor was it discovered in retrospect. We had planned it as part of our strategy. It was the most important thing. The next stage could wait.

Negotiations for our positive behaviour management policy took a long time, probably two years, but it was time well spent. We had in-service training; a volunteer staff committee produced the draft policy; there were lengthy consultations with all staff, pupils, governors and parents before it was launched. The policy is firmly rooted in our code of conduct, which commits us to respect for each other, ourselves, learning, and the environment. It was also committed at the onset to a target of six rewards to one sanction. The 'log' reveals that this target was exceeded recently; figures for 2000 were 14 rewards to one sanction. The policy, once agreed, was explained fully to small groups of pupils, one group at a time. A feature of this explanation was that we explained that the policy applied to every one working in the school, and the head explained the rewards and sanctions, equating permanent exclusion with dismissal, which applied to staff as well as to pupils. This was regarded as radical but we do not see why it should be. It helped pupils understand that school mirrored the world of work in this. We asked all parents to sign to indicate their agreement with the policy on their child's entrance to school, with 100 per cent success.

It is interesting to note that staff, parents and governors believe that the new Home–School agreement that we have been instructed to put in place, according to strict government guidelines, is a far weaker instrument than our former practice of getting parents and pupils to sign up to the behaviour policy. Another downside of being a little ahead of the game.

Target practice

The rise in GCSE results surprised us: we had hoped for 20 per cent and got 27 per cent A*–C grades. We still treasure the letter received from the then Chief Inspector of Schools, Chris Woodhead, in reply to the head's rather tetchy enquiry as to why we were not one of his 100 best schools when we had almost trebled, not doubled, our examination results in two years and had a positive Ofsted report. He said he was deeply appreciative of the work we were doing and would consider us for next year, but we were not on the first list because the results and the Ofsted inspection had occurred in two different academic years. Consider us next year? What were we supposed to do? Get 81 per cent A*–Cs and ask Ofsted back?

The A*–G grades were over 90 per cent too. So we decided as a management team that we would set targets in advance of government requirements, and publish these to governors. Setting the targets was done in a rather vague way, we must admit, and we did not get down to pupil level. The long-term target was that by 2001 we would hope to ensure that no individual department's results were lower than the current best-performing department in 1996. We have not got there yet. We also expected departments to set targets, and these were interesting and very honestly done, especially as these, too, went to governors. Heads of department committed themselves to things such as 'establishing a better work ethos so that more pupils are entered for GCSE' and 'getting more As'. Some did put more formal numbers on it, with varying means of justification. Actually, it was not a bad way to start. With some prompting from the deputy head (achievement) – an unusual title in 1994 – heads of department were to analyse where their weaknesses lay as well as their strengths.

Results rose to 30 per cent A*–Cs in 1996, but it was a 'good year'. The next year held, and it had been a problematical cohort. With that came a new school confidence from the staff. One set of good results could be a fluke, repeating these results with another cohort, perceived as of less ability, meant that their teaching had made a difference. It was a heady time. We plateaued at 30 per cent for the next year, then went up to 34 per cent and 36 per cent. Pupil numbers grew. We began to believe that continuous improvement was possible. As a staff we had, in fact, swallowed our own propaganda. Which was fine.

Disillusionment

In 1998, the head was seconded for eight months to work in the LEA acting as chief education officer (head of Education Services then in Barnsley) during an interregnum. This delayed the next big push to get a teaching and learning policy in place, as the newly appointed staff development officer, Sue Simmons, had to undertake additional duties. This post was re-evaluated by the governors in 1999 to deputy head (teaching and learning), again somewhat in advance of common practice. We already knew we had to move ahead again quickly.

But the standards agenda had, at last, caught up with us. The pressure from above, from government and Ofsted; the LEA waking up to the realities of accountability for LEA targets and applying their own pressure; the looming performance management and threshold perceived as a threat by teachers; the tales from failing schools; in short, the sense of fear that had begun to permeate the profession began to take its toll. The that strategic agenda began to be identified in the minds of some staff with the government's standards agenda – with hindsight, we see that this caused some disillusionment.

When we advertised for a new deputy head (achievement) in the summer of 2000, the head's briefing to governors included the following statement:

As governors are aware, the school is at an important turning point.

Academic results have improved consistently over the last few years, attendance and behaviour are also greatly improved. The school environment is attractive and well maintained and after years of having to count every penny, we are at last in a position to make additional teaching and non teaching appointments. The ICT provision for the school is now more than adequate, and if things go to plan, should be very good soon.

The next stage, which will take some years, is to break the '40 per cent barrier' in terms of pupils achieving more than five A*–C grades, while maintaining the breadth of achievement which is a matter of pride to the school and above national average. To do this we shall be concentrating on the following areas:

- *progression from Key Stage 2 to Key Stage 3;*
- *progression within Key Stage 3;*
- *review of the homework policy;*
- *major review of the curriculum in 2000–2001;*
- *obtaining more grades at A and B level, GCSE;*
- *realistic and rigorous target setting for individual pupils throughout the school;*
- *development of a teaching and learning policy;*
- *creative work with pupils in school who are 'at risk' of social exclusion.*

The school agenda is firmly rooted in the national agenda of social inclusion, access for all to education, commitment to learning, professional standards for teachers, the concept of continuous improvement and clear target setting for both students and staff. We want a colleague who fully understands the national picture and who will work within the school leadership group to shape the future of this school in the context of national aspirations.

A huge agenda! One, nonetheless, that we were prepared to tackle with confidence.

When, however, we advertised for a new deputy head (teaching and learning) in November 2000 for an Easter 2001 appointment, the head included the following statement:

The last of these (creative work with pupils in school who are 'at risk' of social exclusion) has very recently assumed even greater importance as we are beginning to see a substantial increase in 'pupil turbulence' with a significant influx of pupils with either serious attendance problems or patterns of disruptive behaviour, from other schools. This is a particular problem when they enter the school in KS4.

The person appointed will play a leading role in school improvement through standards of teaching and learning and the management of teacher performance. Strategies to engage these often-difficult pupils, who come to us without the support of our positive ethos from Year 7, will form an important part of the teaching and learning agenda.

We need, therefore, to appoint a person capable of strong leadership and one who has a firm grasp of the elements of good teaching and an understanding of different learning styles. Equally important is the ability to communicate these to others and work with teachers in a supportive, not threatening, manner.

The person appointed will need considerable skills in dealing with both teaching and non-teaching staff. We do not have time to waste in unprofitably lengthy debate, but equally, everyone involved must be made to feel that they have been consulted and are fully 'on board'.

The addition was significant and reflected a new pattern, posing a threat to school improvement for all except the fortunately situated schools.

When the head and the newly appointed deputy (achievement), Chris Wilson, worked on the statutory targets for 2002/2003 they discovered a surprising anomaly. The Key Stage 3 SATs results for the 2000–2001 Year 10 cohort were the best the school had ever had, and predicted a possible attainment at GCSE of 40 per cent A*–C grades and 96 per cent A*–G grades. Promising but challenging, we thought. But the Year 11 information service (YELLIS) scores for the same year predicted a rather worrying 27 per cent A*–Cs. This made no sense. Remember, however, that the SATs were taken in May 2000 and the YELLIS tests in October of the same year. When we tracked the difference we discovered that a significant number of pupils had come into Year 10 since September, almost all with poor records of attendance, behavioural problems, a history of permanent exclusion and, in some cases, very challenging behaviour. We were, in fact, not looking at the same cohort at all. And the list of pupils wanting to enter the current Year 10 continues to grow: partly because of circumstances, including the fact that several local schools are 'full', partly because we have a reputation for being able to manage difficult pupils.

Chris and the head agreed on the following strategy: they would set the targets mid-way between the two pieces of performance data evidence. In other words, they would split the difference and tell the LEA that we would aim for a conversion rate of the incoming pupils of 50 per cent success in examinations. The LEA agreed. The governors agreed too, but registered their concern at the phenomenon.

An ongoing struggle

There are other effects of this growing 'turbulence': the Pupil Retention Grant funds depend on reducing exclusions. Our exclusion rate is low. If we permanently exclude more than three pupils this year, we will lose funds at the rate of £3000 a time. If we had started from, say, ten per year, we would be in a more secure position financially.

More insidiously, litter is beginning to creep back into the school, minor damage is occurring in the grounds. The ethos is not taking a 'fix' on the incoming pupils quickly enough, and a few – but a significant few – of our 'original' pupils are following the wrong lead.

But we press on because we really believe in doing a quality job for our pupils and raising achievement. Since September 2001 Chris Wilson has led the introduction of a reporting system for parents, in which teachers set three individual targets for each child in each subject. There will be an interim report as well, computer-generated, to provide parents with statistical information, carefully explained. Chris has also incorporated mentoring time into a full curriculum review (which took two months from start to finish) for implementation in September 2001, and training will be given to staff on mentoring skills. We are not standing still. The newly appointed deputy head (teaching and learning) Dave Sim will have to move fairly smartly, too. We need that teaching and learning policy.

But the truth is that there is a price. The leadership group is working flat out, arriving very early and/or staying very late. The assistant head (individual needs), David Parkes, has quietly (but valiantly) been picking up parts of all the senior managers' jobs for the past three years, during the head's secondment, three long-term absences and two interregnums. Teachers feel, urgently, the need for classroom support with this group of 'turbulent' (in every sense) pupils who have not absorbed the ethos of the school and see respect and tolerance as weakness to be challenged. It takes more time and money – we have invested in allowances for staff to act as integration tutor and pupil support plan tutor; added an assistant special educational needs co-ordinator (SENCO); employed a full-time counsellor on a high salary and created a base for her. We are doing everything we can.

We are also older. Wiser and still creative, perhaps, but still physically older as a staff.

One of the problems facing us is that, as a leadership group, we continue to drive forward the strategic agenda we set out in 1994 but in very different circumstances. Then we were led by hope and pride, and a belief that anything was possible with our staff and our children. The standards agenda has followed us and overshadowed our bright optimism, bringing a new sense of external compulsion from which school leaders find it very difficult to protect staff. Though they must.

You cannot compel love. And it is love that informs any human achievement of real and lasting worth. Teachers now feel that they are being *made* to do the things that they once did from their hearts, for the children, and this is not good. It is also very difficult to manage successfully, though we are trying.

We have lost to early retirement good teachers at every level from deputy to main professional scale. It should not be like this. If school improvement is to be sustainable, then the people who make the improvements possible, the teachers and school leaders, must feel appreciated, safe and above all confident to take the risks that are essential to creativity, whether institutional or personal in the day-to-day teaching.

A final irony is that the staff of this school are about to watch other schools gaining performance awards – because we have improved so far, it is difficult to imagine our meeting any criteria for these. When so many will be recognised, it is hard for our teachers to accept that they have never been publicly thanked for the work they have done in the past.

The standards agenda is with us to stay; in one sense rightly so. No teacher should ever deliver to their pupils any lesser quality of service than they would wish for their own child; that means the best educational chance possible. Less than the best cannot do. But the authors are glad that Wombwell was ahead of the standards agenda; that we made our improvements because we wanted to, because we cared, and because we worked together as a school to do it. And we are going to stay to see it through the next stage.

5

■ ■ ■

Restructuring Around Learning

by Geoff Barton and Mike Foley

We begin with a morality tale. The Whitehall Study (1999) followed more than 30 000 civil servants for 30 years to study patterns of health and premature death. The civil service was chosen because it was such a hierarchical structure and would enable researchers to see what effect rank could have on your chances of survival into old age. Who would be most likely to die prematurely – the Sir Humphrey-style mandarin at the top of the civil service tree or the lowly doorman with little stress or responsibility?

The answer, of course, was the doorman. The researchers found that the key factors influencing your physical and mental health are neither your genes nor your behaviour – whether you smoke or drink, take exercise or eat fatty foods; these factors together account for less than four out of ten premature deaths. What really ensures good health is the efficiency of our fight or flight response, the way our hormones rise and fall in response to perceived physical threat. The results of the Whitehall Study show that what determines this is the amount of control you have over your everyday life.

So this explains the increased survival rate of senior civil servants – four times more likely to reach normal age expectancy compared with a clerk on the lowest rung. Senior civil servants may have to carry the burden of responsibility and experience the stress of life at the top, but they do at least have control. People who have low job control face a 50 per cent higher risk of new illness: heart attacks, stroke, diabetes or merely ordinary infection.

What value is this study to the way that we run schools? Our work at Thurston Community College near Bury St Edmunds in Suffolk over the past three years has focused on ways of stripping away hierarchical structures and reaffirming the skills and talents of students and teachers at all levels. There is always something rhetorical about this kind of statement, and we shy away from grand claims of empowerment and liberation. Our starting point is more humble: schools are often large organisations in which the individual – child or adult – can feel lost or uninvolved or insignificant.

We were motivated by a view that rigidly hierarchical structures are based on a 19th-century view of industrial control, something our early strategic work with Professor John West-Burnham had been useful in highlighting. All too often, as others have pointed out, schools are managed within a structure more appropriate for a cotton mill or prison, a kind of 'control the workers' set-up. We believe that teachers are highly skilled (if often under-confident) professionals who would work better with greater autonomy, more personal control of their situation, and fewer management layers. Our experience of many new colleagues entering the profession is the extent of their idealism and passion for the enterprise of teaching. And then what happens? In too many cases the structures and expectations of a school environment stifle such optimism.

The question was whether we could make a school setting – almost by definition an environment of control and authority – more genuinely rewarding as a learning environment for teacher and student. This chapter describes the starting point of that transformation process: a restructuring that is just beginning.

The two thrusts of our work are about students and teachers: how can we bring the individual learning needs of the student to the fore, and how can we give autonomy and accountability to small, tight-knit teaching teams?

Focus one: student learning

It has become a platitude to ask teachers to compare two images of teaching, one from the early 21st century, the other from the early 20th century. What differences are there – the clothing, the fashion for moustaches, the electric sockets in the wall? Many other apparent essentials – from groups of children in serried ranks, to teacher in authoritarian pose, to blackboard – will have stayed the same in many establishments. And while there is much to be said for the didactic model of teacher/pupil, none of our reading convinces us that learning always has to take place in a context of one adult to 30 students in a room with desks. In other words, we have been seeking ways of individualising the teaching and learning process, with a particular emphasis on learning about learning.

Thurston is a large school with about 1300 students. The disparate rural catchment area – some 550 square kilometres – means that most students arrive and leave by bus. This makes any ideals about extending the school day to incorporate breakfast learning and twilight sessions difficult and expensive.

Originally organised into three houses, led by the heads of house, this was a fairly monolithic structure. Being part of a house still left many students feeling like a small fish in a large pond. Our aim was to modernise the student experience, but not through some neat paper restructuring that would look elegant and reassuring but alter little in the day-to-day dynamic of teaching and learning. We wanted to effect change that would fundamentally alter what it is like to be a student in a large institution. Creating smaller teams was central to this. We broke the three houses into six, gave them new names, and created student committees to help develop an ethos.

But that's not really so far removed from the public school tradition, from the world of Harry Potter. The real challenge is to reinvent school using the most positive aspects of our modern, consumer-orientated age. And this is where many teachers start to become twitchy. The culture of schools and 'the world out there' have often seemed in opposition, often impressively so. At their best, schools can feel (for adult and child) like a sanctuary from a brutal, unforgiving world beyond the perimeter fence. But they can also feel unreal, artificial environments, unlikely genuinely to prepare some students for the next phase of their lives.

Our knee-jerk reaction as teachers, from within the cosy confines of the public sector, is that the consumer society, the world of survivalist market forces, must automatically be bad. It leaves the weak vulnerable; it exercises no moral judgement; it embodies bad taste. But this is such an unhelpfully simplistic view. Consumerism has created an astonishing world of personal choice. From supermarket diversity to digital services, we can customise our world to suit our tastes, interests and lifestyle. And this is the brave new world our students inhabit. It is a place full of the promise that being an individual – 'be yourself' – is the all-important totem. And yet the forces of marketing exhort us all the time to change who we are, to reinvent ourselves.

This astringent consumerism is seductively compelling to our students, and if schools fail to respond in some degree then we believe that an increasing number of students – now able to access individualised learning programmes through computer technology – will regard school as redundant or irrelevant.

Most teachers, of course, will take a more critical stance, dismissive of the shallowness of a media culture, and concerned that an emphasis on individual rights appears to have little place for personal responsibility; concerned also at the moral vacuum that a world of 'me, me, me' creates. We would argue that the school's role is educating students about – but not *against* – the values of a consumer world. Our challenge, in other words, is to create ways for schools – traditionally concerned with the social control of large numbers – to revitalise the importance of individuals and their learning needs. The aim is to trust students to know best how and when they learn, to grant them more autonomous control of their own learning. Howard Gardner's ground-breaking work on multiple intelligences, Alistair Smith's models of accelerated learning – these remind us that the single model of the student-in-class is no longer holding true.

Our aim is to build a customer-focused concept of education in which students more actively shape their own learning programme. Our personal, health and social education (PHSE) programme in the student's first term now teaches about brain theory and how to apply that to learning. Students learn about multiple intelligences and mind-mapping. Sixth-form students join main school tutor groups to help them review progress and get them involved in school life. Each student is expected to take on a whole-school role. Year 11 students can opt for lunchtime workshops, one-to-one revision coaching with another students. The school intranet provides study and support materials. Our Parent Teacher Association (PTA) has been refocused to run sessions showing parents how they can best support their child's learning.

We also concur with much of the thrust of recent work on literacy. This is predicated on the notion that implicit language skills – the ability to listen, read, speak and write – often need to be made more explicit if students are to employ them more effectively. So, ask a child to write the opening of a thriller and you'll get a range of responses. Those from bookish backgrounds are more likely to use an appropriate range of stylistic effects. The others may or may not. Spend time drawing out the essential ingredients of thrillers – the attention to mood, the way structure can build suspense, the role of dialogue in building character – and you start to see more informed and successful writing. In the same way, many of our students speak inappropriately to adults not through intention but through a lack of appropriate frameworks and models. They are not familiar with the modes by which a student might, for example, make a complaint or ask for clarification. Resorting to gut instinct can lead to accusations of rudeness or insolence. Some of our students therefore need more explicit work on social skills, on how to hold conversations with adults.

We now aim to be much more explicit in our expectations of students, not just in terms of behaviour but in providing models of success. From their arrival in school, students are given a map of essential ingredients – the skills and qualities we have identified as characteristics of our most successful students. Referred to in assemblies, PHSE, tutor time and on posters around school, this list of 'student essentials' provides students with a template for success – a tangible guide to how to do better at school.

There is nothing significantly radical about this, but the reassurance and clarity it brings to students appears to be appreciated.

Learning

A successful student is one who can demonstrate that they know how to learn, knows the sort of learner they are and how to work in a variety of ways. To be able to do this you will need the following skills and qualities:

- *have high expectations of the quality of work you will produce;*
- *be motivated;*
- *use target setting to improve the quality of the work you produce;*
- *be able to meet deadlines;*
- *be able to carry out independent research;*
- *evaluate strengths and weaknesses to improve your learning in future;*
- *concentration;*
- *be able to develop areas of special interest.*

Personal qualities

To be able to create a community that works and learns together you will need the following qualities both in your time at Thurston and in the workplace:

- *courtesy;*
- *trustworthiness and reliablity;*
- *commitment;*
- *adaptability – ability to cope with change;*
- *having a broad range of interests, e.g. sport/social, life/academic/cultural aspects – books, music, films, art, etc.;*
- *be able to make informed decisions;*
- *be able to plan and organise your own workload;*
- *be able to value your own and other people's individuality.*

Knowledge

There are certain areas that you will need to have some knowledge of if you are going to be able to make important life decisions for yourself. These are:

- *nutrition and healthy eating;*
- *diseases and preventative medicine;*
- *importance of exercise;*
- *facts about drugs;*
- *contraception and sexually transmitted diseases;*
- *mental health;*
- *personal finances;*
- *criminal justice system;*
- *political awareness;*
- *awareness of opportunities and careers;*
- *first aid.*

Citizenship

Citizenship is the way in which society works together to achieve certain common goals. These help our world to run efficiently and encourage people to be able to live and work together showing mutual respect. You will be able to show that you are a good citizen by:

- *participation in school life, e.g. house committees, sports teams, orchestras, debating society, etc.;*
- *contributing to school life, e.g. helping out in departments, charity committees, school council, contributing to assemblies, etc.;*
- *being involved in the local community, e.g. helping the elderly, play groups, primary schools, local charities, youth clubs, etc.;*
- *ability to discuss issues in the news;*
- *ability to express political views;*
- *ability to demonstrate some understanding of local politics.*

Coupled with all of this we see the need for a vibrant programme of assemblies and tutorial work which reinforces core values all the time – an emphasis on responsibility, courtesy and learning.

The tutorial programme for our sixth formers is driven by the six key skills, with special emphasis on the so-called 'soft' key skills of problem solving, working with others, and managing your own learning. These provide the framework for students to take control of their learning, identify the essential skills they need to develop, and provide the basis for an informed discussion with their tutor or, in more and more cases, learning mentor.

From September, these key skills will also drive our PHSE programme, providing a core of skills and experiences to help students make connections between fragmented school experiences and become more involved in controlling their own learning.

This has been the process by which we have begun to refocus the school on principles of learning. At the same time, more challengingly, we knew we had to change the staffing structures within which the learning is managed. Hence our second area of focus.

Focus two: teachers teaching

Most schools remain hierarchical structures with layers of management. The proliferation of legislation in the 1980s and 1990s led to enlarged senior management teams and a host of management allowances being awarded for implementation of new initiatives, often divorced from the core business of improving learning. Thurston Community College differed little from other schools in this respect. It had a large senior team – headteacher, three deputies, business manager and up to four senior teachers. The size of the team might have been justified in terms of its size – 1300 students – but the question we had to answer was whether it was the most effective way of taking the school forward into the 21st century.

Interestingly, Thurston had missed out on the trend towards faculties which dominated most staffing change in the 1980s. Consequently the middle management layer consisted of an array of heads of department, mainly being paid on an historical pay spine. Meetings at this level often topped 30 or 40 colleagues, with little hope of doing real work or arriving at a decision. They tended to follow a similar pattern: senior team makes a proposal; proposal is presented to 36 middle managers; discussion follows, sometimes leading to dissent; initiative falls to the wayside or gets implemented with middle managers complaining that consultative management style is a sham.

In a survey of staff carried out in conjunction with Eastern Electricity in 1997, staff clearly stated their perception that they were not consulted and were not part of the decision-making process. They believed they had little or no control over what happened to them in their daily work, which led to low morale and lack of motivation.

The view from the bridge was somewhat different. There was a lack of trust in middle managers, an unwillingness to place responsibility and decision making lower down in the hierarchy in case it went wrong. This in turn led to greater dependency on the part of classroom teachers and middle managers who referred minor and even trivial matters to members of the senior team. Not surprisingly, it resulted in frustration all round and the grinding prospect of one relatively small wheel trying to turn a much larger one with maximum resistance.

The task was to introduce a new structure that would move us away from this deeply embedded culture. Our aims were:

- to give curriculum areas control over their work in order to raise motivation and release the creativity that undoubtedly exists among a talented staff;
- to strip away the layers of management that had built up over the years so that there was a clear line of responsibility;
- to make the head of curriculum areas – whom we have called team leaders – directly responsible for the quality of learning and the performance of staff;
- to reduce the leadership group to four and ensure that they are primarily concerned with strategic planning and implementation;
- to build a new management team responsible for 'cranking' the school up every morning and guaranteeing that it runs efficiently;
- to give wide-ranging powers to middle managers and devolve as much money as possible to team leaders to spend on improving learning.

We also wished to blur the unhelpful distinctions that have dogged many schools – the division between teachers and 'non-teachers' (what a phrase that is!). Once you place the learning process firmly at the heart of the education process, the old dichotomy falls away. Our network manager is involved in the education process as much as our new science teacher.

The new staffing structure, a strongly non-hierarchical model which places the teaching teams at the core, is shown in Figure 5.1. This represents a shift away from a heavily hierarchical model. It emphasises flexibility and shared goals, and a blurring of the distinction between teaching and support staff. Teaching and learning is firmly at its heart as the core purpose of everyone working at Thurston Community College.

Leadership group: This is the core team who, working with governors, drives school strategy. It will comprise of the head, two deputies and a business manager. Linked to the annual planning process, other colleagues may be invited to join the leadership group to help take the lead on particular initiatives.

Figure 5.1 The new staffing structure at Thurston Community College from September 2001

Teaching team leaders:	This is the significant role for whole-school curriculum planning, maintaining and developing the ethos of the school, raising the quality of teaching and learning, and developing staff skills. This team, with the curriculum and assessment managers, will form the new curriculum committee.
Heads of house:	This is the key role for monitoring student performance across subjects, for ensuring an ethos of high achievement, and for developing students' skills beyond the academic.
Management team:	This team has responsibility for the day-to-day management of the school – administration manager, business manager, *et al.*
Learning support team:	This is the group whose focus on learning embraces such essential skills as literacy, numeracy, information retrieval and individual support. It incudes special needs, inclusion, mentoring, librarian and learning support assistants. The team is a combination of teaching and support staff – part of our aim to blur such distinctions.

At the heart of the new structure are the team leaders. The post of head of faculty, which many schools introduced in the 1980s, was curriculum-led. Most heads of science, humanities and performing arts were appointed to introduce combined courses. It was an attempt to patch up the fragmentation of the curriculum, but had little to do with performance or quality of learning.

The new teaching team leader post at Thurston is not designed to do this, although the hope is that it will lead to greater co-operation and consistency across the curriculum. The role of the team leader in this model is quite different. We wish to develop a group of middle managers who take full responsibility for the quality of learning in their teams. They will need to have a detailed knowledge of the strengths and weaknesses in their area which has come about from regular conversation, observation, and systematic evaluation of data.

We will expect team leaders to know how the team has performed:

- across all grades;
- among the highest and lowest achievers;
- with different student groups (boys/girls/free school meals/different levels of prior achievement, for example);
- across different elements of the assessment (coursework/exam/different attainment targets);
- within different teaching groups;
- actual against predicted grades.

We will expect them to know how they compare:

- with the national average;
- with national benchmark figures;
- with Local Education Authority averages;
- with local comparator departments;
- with trends over time;
- with other subjects within the school.

Finally, we will expect team leaders to monitor the progress of individual students to ensure that they make the expected progress.

Once key areas for improvement have been identified, team leaders will be empowered to draw up their own plans for improvement in line with the budgets that have been given to them. Budgets will exist for consultancy and advice, training, supply (to enable team teaching and observation to take place), as well as the traditional 'pot' for capitation. In due course, budgets will also exist for staffing and for furniture and fabric.

Accountability will be focused on the outcomes, both quantitative and qualitative. The deputy head responsible for line-managing the seven team leaders will ensure that targets are consistent with the whole-school improvement plan and, through regular one-to-one meetings, that they are progressing according to plan.

How might it work in practice?

Take the example of the geography department, which finds that less able boys are underachieving at General Certificate of Secondary Education (GCSE). The humanities team agrees that this is a major priority. Students say that the assignments are poorly presented and the fieldwork carried out in the local village fails to motivate them. Above all, they receive little support because departmental policy is for coursework to be done at home. Poor coursework results quickly convince them that it is not worth making much effort with other parts of the course.

The team leader decides to offer an allowance to a member of staff to lead the project for improvement. Money is set aside to attend exam meetings and some of the supply budget will be used for observation and team teaching. The team leader will call the headteacher of a neighbouring school that is achieving particularly good geography results at GCSE. She will invite the head of geography from that school to lead some in-service education and training (INSET) at a departmental meeting. She is willing to pay preparation fees, travel fees and the cost of cover.

Targets have been approved by the deputy head: 98 per cent of all boys will complete the geography GCSE course through to final examination, average coursework marks for less able boys will reach at least 50 per cent, and all coursework assignments will be completed. The findings from the geography project will be shared with other team leaders, since boys' underachievement is a whole school issue.

At the same time the team have decided to spend their furniture budget on murals and display boards in the humanities block. The displays will contain student work that has been specially annotated to provide exemplars of good work. The furniture budget is particularly healthy because everyone is taking more responsibility for the fabric of the building.

Within this new framework, much is expected of the team leaders. Initially, they will teach for two-thirds of the week. They will have administrative support to enable them to concentrate on pedagogy and improvement. This support will be deployed as they see fit – for stock, exam entries, organisation of orals or the French exchange, or possibly contact with parents and employers.

The investment in team leaders over the next three years will be immense. They will need to be highly trained in self-evaluation, action planning, project management, budget control, personnel management and the latest research on learning. We are determined to invest in personal coaching so that each team leader is able to reach the high standards that we expect.

The outcomes for the school will be improved communication, swift decision making, true empowerment, and a culture of continuous improvement in learning.

This process is not fundamentally about structures and diagrams. It is about ethos. Our aim is to change expectations of what it is like to be a student and to be a teacher, and to challenge many of the old assumptions about ways of working. But working practices are difficult to shift without new models, and for this reason our revitalisation of the pastoral system – rooted in showing students how to be successful learners – and our reconceptualising of teaching teams are about shifting attitudes and improving motivation. Changing structures, in other words, is an important route to changing ethos.

We always said that learning was at the heart of what we do. Now symbolically and in practice it has to be. On this we will be judged.

References

Gardner, H. (1984) *Frames of Mind: the theory of multiple intelligences*. New York: Basic Books.

Smith, A. (1998) *Accelerated Learning in Practice*. Stafford: Network Educational Press.

Marmot, M. and Wilkinson, R. (1999) *The Social Determinants of Health*, Oxford: Oxford University Press.

6
■ ■ ■

Leaders Making the Difference in Greenford

by Kate Griffin

Introducing Greenford High School

Greenford High School isn't even one century old – it was opened in 1939 by Middlesex County Council as a grammar school for 450 pupils. Greenford is typical of the small localities that were developing to meet the needs of the ever-increasing population of outer London and it is now situated within the London Borough of Ealing; in fact, it is on the borders of Southall and Greenford (however, our position within the Heathrow corridor is one that appears to be more readily recognised).

At the beginning the school was fortunate in being built in the style of the times, i.e. the main building looks like a miniature 'Hoover Building', and was particularly well endowed in terms of the extensive playing fields, albeit on poorly drained Middlesex clay. Over the years, however, the surrounding areas have grown and merged so that now it is difficult to identify the boundaries of particular places and they have few individual characteristics that would serve to give them an identity. In 1974 the school became a comprehensive for 12–18-year-olds and over time buildings were added to accommodate the increasing roll.

It is Southall that gives the school its predominant characteristics. Southall is the centre of an established Asian community, which planted its roots here in the 1950s. Southall High Street provides a key to the flavour of our community, with its exotic food and fabric shops and mixture of cultures. Although there is a tremendous variety of languages, signs are written mostly in English and Punjabi. The majority of our students are of Asian origin and almost all are drawn from this local area; in fact most of them live within two kilometres of our gates. There are other groups that have grown in more recent years and which are represented in the school, including those of Somali, Arabic and Afro-Caribbean descent. To direct you to the school I would start with the Target Roundabout on the A40 about two kilometres away but have to say that the public house that gave the roundabout its name is now a McDonald's!

In 1990, the LEA proposed that the organisational structure of its schools should be changed so that the age of transfer would be lowered from 12 to 11 and the sixth forms in LEA-maintained schools would be closed and replaced by a tertiary college. The two voluntary-aided schools would retain their sixth forms and the tertiary college would be located in existing buildings in various parts of the authority. Those consulted were very much in favour of lowering the age of transfer to 11 and their support for this aspect of the plan disguised the amount of opposition to the closing of the sixth forms. The advent of grant-maintained schools at this time offered the opportunity to retain them. Eight of the schools held ballots, six of which were in favour of seeking grant-maintained status. Five were approved by the Secretary of State. Greenford's experience was particularly interesting. The parents petitioned for a ballot, but the governors voted 16 to 2 against the proposal. The first ballot was in favour but without the required turnout, while the second was also in favour and the turnout increased. It was between ballots that I was appointed as headteacher. Together with all the secondary schools in Ealing we admitted Year 7 pupils for the first time in September 1993.

A poor start

So what was the situation at Greenford when I joined in 1991? The school had already changed from having a predominantly white intake to one with a majority of pupils coming from the Indian subcontinent. The number on the roll was 800, with 145 in the sixth form. Twenty per cent of Year 11 achieved five or more A–C grades at General Certificate of Secondary Education (GCSE); results at A-level were so poor they were not mentioned publicly. The teachers were clearly disappointed by the results, but there seemed to be an acceptance that this level of achievement was all you could expect.

In my first years it was important to ensure that all of us working in the school developed a common understanding of the tasks ahead. Clearly we wanted to improve our results, and in the first stages this was relatively easy as we were coming from such a low base. A look at differentials, a sharing of all the data and the introduction of a Year 11 mentoring programme all helped. I was also convinced that as the parents had been so determined that we should maintain our sixth form, it was vital that there was provision in the sixth form for all our students. So in September 1993, in addition to admitting pupils in Year 7 for the first time, we introduced a wide range of General National Vocational Qualifications (GNVQs) and an access course. This heralded the beginning of our rise in numbers and with this increase the need to appoint considerably more teaching and support staff. By the time of our first inspection in 1994 our number on the roll was 1314, with 218 in the sixth form, and our percentage of students achieving the five or more good grades at GCSE had risen to 33. The inspection team was most impressed that this improvement had not been achieved at the expense of our less academic students, whose results had also improved considerably. The team described our school as having many of the characteristics associated with social disadvantage – a third were entitled to free school meals, many lived with domestic overcrowding, and 79 per cent of our students had English as a second language.

Following that first encouraging inspection (which endorsed our programmes with comments such as 'maintain', 'continue' and 'ensure good practice is spread') it was clear that to continue to improve it was essential that we developed some longer-term strategies to raise achievement. The inspectors had also suggested that we apply for the Investors in People (IIP) award, as they felt that so many of the programmes that we had in place fitted the criteria that we would have to satisfy. The consideration of the IIP criteria reinforced my belief that it would be through staff development and a possible change of structure that we would ensure that our improvements were sustained and provide a platform for development into the 21st century.

The structure that had been in place previously had relied almost exclusively on the head and the three deputies, the role of the senior teachers had been variable, and we were not perceived by the rest of the staff to be a team working together. During my first year in the school I had altered the responsibilities of the three deputy headteachers and some of the senior teachers, but I had not radically altered our way of working. During the course of 1995 one of the deputies decided to take early retirement and two of the senior teachers left. This provided an opportunity to consider changes that previously had been impossible. We had a chance to discuss in detail proposals for a new structure that I hoped would not only support learning and raise achievement for the pupils but would also provide a more enjoyable and supportive way of working. My aim was to develop a model that took account of the views of the existing members of the team while ensuring that the final product provided a secure structure for the school with clear means of communication. Considerable discussion was already taking place around the roles of schools in the future. I believed that schools would have a future, albeit with many, as yet, unknown features. I felt it was critical that the structure of the senior management team provided good role models for both staff and pupils and was designed so that we could respond to change sensibly and quickly.

Most important of all was the need for the structure to support learning throughout the school.

The process

The discussions were obviously going to be very sensitive and there was a danger that if we did not manage to achieve a model that was supported by all involved, a great deal of damage could be done both to the individuals concerned and to the success that had already been achieved. We agreed that the first meeting would take place after school and off site. We used a local hotel and agreed that after the main part of the meeting we would have dinner.

It was an interesting meeting, not least because I learned parts of the history of the school that I had never heard before. We 'went back to basics' and first of all went through a brainstorming session that listed all the roles and responsibilities of a senior management team (SMT). We then used the results of this activity to discuss our roles so that we all shared the same view of the SMT's purpose. I was relieved that very early on in our discussions there was an agreement that any structures we set up must enable the school to operate successfully as a learning organisation. Following the evening session we planned a weekend away, and not only did we agree the programme and the agenda but we also circulated a pack of information that included details of all the current job descriptions, line management structures and even more important a pack of 'a little light reading' from educational thinkers and researchers.

During that weekend we discussed these topics:

- what key roles should be covered by the SMT;
- how do we ensure that there are no grey areas between jobs that mean that tasks are left undone;
- optimum size;
- quality control aspects of the work of the SMT;
- the use of the SMT meeting time;
- links between SMT roles and the School Development Plan (SDP) – this also meant discussing the links to the governing body's committees as each committee takes charge of a strand of the plan;
- monitoring the work of the school;
- sharing good practice.

Throughout all our discussions we tried to ensure that we did not lose sight of the things that were going well. I also kept a note of all the weaknesses mentioned so that when the final system was agreed we were able to check that we had taken steps to improve them. We didn't only think of the make-up and structure of the SMT but also how our working would support and develop the role of middle managers within the school.

As the meeting was held at a weekend it was important that precious time was not wasted. To help keep us on track and ensure that we did not go round in circles, we employed the services of Michael Smith, a consultant from the training and consultancy division of the Secondary Heads Association. He made the following comments about the session:

> *I think that it was very useful to let the outside world into your insider sessions, my being there put a brake on the wilder comments and possibly also stopped some members of the team pushing their own agendas too aggressively. As so often happens in discussions of this sort, people made statements that were assumptions, although they were stated as fact. My ability to question these assumptions ensured that the really factual elements were teased out. I think my contribution was useful as it had the effect of sharpening the exercise.*

The weekend marked a turning point in our progress. Although the actual decisions made were rather limited, the extent of the understanding of each other's positions was such that the next stages were accomplished relatively quickly and painlessly. The external consultant's role was important, not least because at times his points were the ones that we could all disagree with. I would hasten to add that we did not disagree with all that he said! At the end of this session he advised that I should spend a little time considering all the points that had been made and then put forward definite proposals for the way ahead. At subsequent meetings we discussed the advantages and disadvantages of the models I proposed and a final model was agreed that took account of the following points:

- There should be seven members of the team. The head aside, the model would enable three pairs to work closely together. These partnerships were designed not only to increase co-operation but also to provide a mechanism whereby we were more likely to cover an 'under the bus' situation. If the pairs worked closely together to share ideas, then an additional benefit would be to reduce the sense of isolation that sometimes occurs in senior teams.

- The term 'assistant head' should be used instead of senior teacher. We hoped that this term would help to indicate the level of responsibility involved.

- All members of the team would be directly responsible to the headteacher; one of the perceived weaknesses of our existing structure was the time it took to get a decision, and we hoped that the proposed model would enable the middle managers to go directly to the member of the team with the expertise to answer their question. For example, a query about purchasing would go the deputy head (premises and finance), a question about a change of the curriculum on offer would go to the deputy head (pupils).

- The roles should be clearly defined and related entirely to whole school management. We felt it to be very difficult to be both a member of the SMT and at the same time hold a middle management responsibility (for example, a head of house).

- Each member of the team should have a responsibility for a strand of the School Development Plan.

The model I proposed was designed to provide the opportunity for the SMT to work in various groups. However, the underlying partnerships were planned not only to give opportunities for the sharing of expertise and ideas but to save time at our full meetings, as possible difficulties may well have been spotted previously in partnership discussions. I also hoped that the person putting forward a proposal would not feel so defensive of it.

Figure 6.1 illustrates clearly the importance given to raising achievement. We lost the post that was dedicated to research and development but within our discussions we made it quite clear that these aspects needed to be taken into account when carrying out the raising achievement role. The assistant head in charge of post-16 education was placed in the inner circle because it was not anticipated that he would change roles. However, it was agreed at the outset that the assistant heads in the outer circle would move round every two years, the intention being that, by the end of six years, each would have experienced all aspects of school management. At the beginning of every year each pair would decide the exact allocation of responsibilities for that year. In the first cycle the raising achievement role was directed mainly at the sixth form because although we had made considerable progress at Key Stage 4, our post-16 results had not built sufficiently upon that improvement.

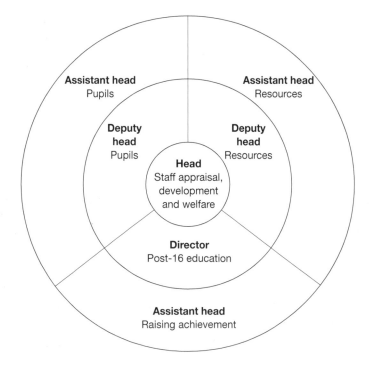

Figure 6.1 Raising achievement

Immediate consequences

We had completed this process, including the meetings we needed to have with governors, by the end of the spring term. Our weekend had taken place in the middle of January and a paper setting out our proposals was circulated on 10 March. It was immediately obvious that these proposals would need to be followed by opportunities for the school's middle managers to be involved in a similar process so that the 'new' thinking could be widely shared. These sessions were helpful and these managers, too, were prepared to take part in a weekend residential. The model was then extended to include them. They responded very well to the idea of more autonomy, and instead of a line manager approach, we adopted a critical friend model to be used only as needed.

Meetings of the senior team were more relaxed and considerably more fun – our greater understanding of each other meant that we could take more risks. In particular, as pairs took responsibility for various initiatives, discussions were less personalised and less territorial. Members of the team reported feeling less isolated.

A new assistant head was appointed to cover resources. Shortly after this appointment we were in a position to outline in considerable detail to a full governing body how we would meet the proposed developments for the following year together with a clear picture of the tasks and the personnel involved.

Last, we introduced a scheme that we hoped would enable staff to communicate more readily with each other. As the school had grown so rapidly, one major concern was that communication was not as good as it had been in the past. Our solution? Coffee in the staff room before school, and coffee and sticky buns in the staff room at break. The health-conscious asked if fruit could be provided as well – so it was.

Two years on

I was reassured to have read that when Professor Mortimer, while in Australia, had heard it suggested that there would not be any 'schools' in the future, as no parent from a home which is rich in learning resources would send a child to a school impoverished in learning resources, he believed this view was wrong:

> My own view is that schools might be different but they will be there. I think the pressures from parents for somewhere safe for young people to go and for young people themselves to get away from their families and meet with their peers will be such that there will always be a form of schooling.
>
> (House of Commons Education and Employment Ninth Report, 1998)

I thought that our structure had proved very supportive to both its members and the school as a whole. We did change roles as planned, but that was not entirely easy. Before the changes were finalised we asked an external appraiser to conduct an appraisal of the work of the team. He consulted widely before drawing up his report and his findings were borne in mind when we changed responsibilities. It is interesting to see how attached people get to their role, and if the office goes with it then it is even harder to prise them away.

However, the examination results continued to improve, particularly at Key Stage 4, and the results in the sixth form were better, although still not as good as we would have liked. The main alteration was in connection with our links with middle managers. The system of critical friends had not worked. We introduced a link member of the SMT for each curriculum area and each house. The attached member was not a line manager, but regular meetings were scheduled so that there were opportunities for discussion on any matter of interest or concern.

Where are we now?

There has been one change to the team, but the model is still working and the school has achieved considerable success. In the summer of 1999, 62 per cent of the Year 11 cohort gained five or more A*–C GCSEs, putting us 25th in the list of most improved schools. We appeared in Her Majesty's Chief Inspector's list of most improved schools in the January 2000 report. In both 1999 and 2000, 98 per cent of Year 11 obtained five or more A*–G grades. In 2000 our percentage achieving five or more A*–C grades dropped to 59 per cent, but we were expecting that. However, we finally managed a real breakthrough in terms of our post-16 results. Our GNVQ results were excellent and of those taking two or more A-levels, 96 per cent passed and our average point score was 18.8. Our roll is now 1540, including 450 in the sixth form.

We have an amazing team of middle managers, classroom teachers and support staff. Some are very young, but their enthusiasm and commitment are outstanding. Having achieved the Investors in People award in 1997 we have now gone successfully through the re-recognition process.

I am convinced that the way in which the SMT is structured and works has played a large part in this success. I am very pleased that, when I said I was writing this chapter and asked for comments, one of our members who has been at Greenford High School since 1974 said: 'I really feel as if I belong, I didn't before.'

Postscript

There are still sticky buns and fruit in the staff room every break, and these do make a difference.

7

■ ■ ■

Quality and Achievement at Hills Road Sixth Form College, Cambridge

by Colin Greenhalgh

The emerging college

The year 2000 saw the centenary of the original foundation of Hills Road Sixth Form College, Cambridge, a good time to take stock of some outstanding achievements in state education and to assess the college's readiness for the challenges of the new century.

The foundation in 1900 established a secondary school for boys with an agricultural bias. Soon after the move to the present site in 1903, academic strengths began to emerge, resulting in the development of a grammar school of some distinction. When comprehensive reorganisation occurred in Cambridgeshire in 1974, the grammar school was the root from which Hills Road Sixth Form College evolved, taking its place in a co-educational system of comprehensive education serving south Cambridgeshire.

There are now more than 1500 sixth-form students, of whom approximately 90 per cent progress to higher education. Since 1990, the A-level pass rate has averaged over 95 per cent, with a substantial proportion of candidates securing the higher grades required by the most competitive universities, including approximately 60 a year who go on to Oxford or Cambridge. Meanwhile, the college's adult programme, launched in 1993, attracts 2500 part-time enrolments a year. A further 1500 members of the local community use the college's sports and tennis centre. Since 1974, the college has cherished the best traditions of its grammar school origins while generating a massive expansion of diverse opportunities which every year benefit several thousand people of all ages.

As the century changed...

Much is owed to the wisdom of the staff who guided the transition from boys' grammar school to co-educational sixth form college. They skilfully identified which formalities of the grammar school tradition should be relinquished cheerfully while maintaining academic rigour, intellectual challenge and a host of enrichment activities outside the classroom. As a result, the new college was an instant success and was soon greatly oversubscribed. Nevertheless, through-out the 1970s and 1980s, neither the college's governors nor the local education authority were willing to contemplate satisfying this demand, not least because the college's buildings, many of them temporary, were barely adequate for the original target of 450 sixth form students. 1990 proved to be a turning point in this respect when the LEA provided new classrooms for biology, geography and history, and the Duke of Edinburgh, as Chancellor of the University of Cambridge, visited the college to perform the opening ceremony.

The popularity and success of the new college gave it the confidence to take full advantage of the dramatic changes in the national educational climate that took place during the last decade of the 20th century. The curricular control imposed by the LEA, resulting in a narrow curriculum base, was loosened by central government decree. The college began to offer a host of new subjects, including art history, business studies, classical civilisation, computing, dance, electronics, geology, human biology, Italian, media studies, music, performing arts, philosophy, photography, political studies, psychology, religious studies, sociology, Spanish, sport studies and physical education. By 2000, students could choose from no fewer than 35 subjects, some of which offered alterna-tive syllabuses. Vocational Advanced Levels in art and design and in business were also introduced. The advent of Curriculum 2000 and the introduction of key skills in application of number, communication and ICT have created even greater breadth in student timetables, which also benefit from the college's long-established programme of enrichment activities.

Sport has always enjoyed a prominent place in the college's life. There are teams in basketball, cricket, equestrian events, hockey, netball, rugby, rowing, soccer, swimming and tennis, with performances of county and national dis-tinction. Drama thrives, partly as a result of the generosity of a former student who gave a theatre to the college, and music making of all kinds involves hun-dreds of students. In recent years students have performed at the National Theatre and at the Royal Festival Hall.

Many college societies attract speakers of international distinction, such as Dr Max Perutz, Professor Stephen Hawking, Lord Alan Bullock and Mr John Major. There are Young Enterprise companies; the Duke of Edinburgh Gold Award scheme; community service activities; fieldwork in biology, geography and geology; residential conferences for artists and historians; foreign exchanges and visits, some of which involve experience of work, in France, Germany, Greece, Italy, Russia, Spain and the USA. This enrichment programme plays an important part in encouraging students to mature into well-rounded adults, developing leadership skills, initiative, enterprise and team working.

The consequences of the Higher and Further Education Act of 1992, which ended the control of the LEA, were profound. The cap on student enrolments and the concept of a defined catchment area were abolished. The college became responsible for its own destiny, seizing with enthusiasm and enterprise the opportunity to develop and to diversify. New buildings, which won a Queen's Anniversary Prize and resulted from an imaginative creation of public and private partnerships, have provided first-class specialist facilities and equipment, including networked ICT throughout the college. The excellence of the buildings and facilities resulted in the Open University and the Open College of the Arts establishing study centres at the college.

Restructuring college leadership

The expansion and diversification of the college's role and activities required radical changes in the senior management structure, which now comprises the principal and the deputy principal (the latter being responsible for curriculum planning and staff development), three assistant principals and a director of resources. One assistant principal is responsible for sixth-form admissions, support and guidance; another leads in the areas of adult education and enterprise; the third is responsible for strategic planning and quality assurance. The director of resources, the most senior member of the support staff, oversees estates, finance and personnel matters. Two curriculum directors manage a traditional departmental structure, the college's view being that a comparatively large number of subject specialists will lead and inspire subject teachers and students more effectively than a smaller number of non-teaching managers. Another vital aspect of middle management is the six senior tutors. They lead teams of personal tutors who are the first point of reference for students and parents, seeing their tutees daily for registration, for dissemination of information and for individual support and guidance.

Strategic planning and quality assurance

The rapidly growing size and diversity of the college's student body, central government's ever greater demands for efficiency and accountability, and the increasingly high expectations of parents and students have posed considerable challenges. The college has responded by adopting new strategic planning and quality assurance processes through which it has addressed with vision and enterprise a number of crucial questions about the nature of its work:

- How should independence be used to manage the future development of the college in a period of rapid change and substantial expansion of student numbers?
- What must the college do to ensure that, like a well-cut diamond, it reflects quality from every angle?
- How can the college provide a full range of high-quality learning experiences responsive to students' needs and leading to achievements that reflect the potential of each individual?
- How can the college evaluate the quality of its work against independent, transparent and comparative criteria?

In responding to these questions, staff at Hills Road have developed significant leadership skills and qualities, including vision, strategic judgement, inspiration, persuasiveness, clarity, consistency, teamwork and valuing the work of others.

People and process

A successful strategic planning process should be inclusive, involving governors, teaching staff, support staff, students, parents, other local schools and colleges, and various interests in the local community. The vision that informs the college's strategic plan is based on the fundamental educational concepts of equality of opportunity, high-quality student experience, and achievement of individual student potential. The vision has been pursued through strategic aims that define the college's mission and translate into specific targets. Some targets are whole-college and others relate to particular areas of the college's work. All members of staff play a key role in the teamwork needed to pursue these targets, the achievement of which determines whether the well-cut diamond is a genuinely apposite image in the eyes of students, parents and the local community.

The principal and others with major responsibilities for leadership have persuaded colleagues of the value of such strategic planning and teamwork. A key argument is the attraction of being part of a successful team which enjoys high public esteem and security of employment. A college that is not advancing is likely to be declining, there being few opportunities for a steady-state existence in contemporary society. Another key challenge for the leadership of the college was to view positively such independent indicators of performance as surveys of student and parental opinion, criteria for Investors in People status, and outcomes of inspections.

Commitment to quality

What factors have enabled the college to face independent judgements with confidence? Some of the most important educational aims – the development of an enquiring mind, an increasing awareness of social responsibility, the growth of self-esteem and of personal confidence – are extremely difficult to measure objectively. Their significance may only become apparent over a life-time. Nevertheless, it is often rightly said that a college that is strongly committed to such objectives is likely to have a distinctive ethos and atmos-phere – a stimulating buzz of excitement in learning and a warmth in human relationships – which are immediately apparent. Many visitors have been kind enough to pay the college this kind of compliment.

As for more tangible aims, the most crucial factor is the certainty that staff and students are performing well. The creation of high-profile quality assurance arrangements, led by a senior member of staff and fed by management infor-mation systems, has revolutionised the possibilities of self-knowledge. Unfortunately, the best known example of management data is the league tables published by central government and national newspapers. Even those schools and colleges that regularly lead the league tables will acknowledge that in present form they provide a distorted snapshot of achievement. Apart from a number of methodological anomalies in their compilation, the tables tend to favour schools and colleges that are selective and well resourced. Nevertheless, year-on-year comparisons can be valuable in plotting trends and the mere exis-tence of the tables begs important questions. For example, what happens to rank order if added value, value for money or other considerations inform the basis of calculations? And what implications do such questions have for the level of allocation of resources to state schools and colleges?

Raising performance using accurate data

Beneath the headline figures of league tables of raw examination results, there are other benchmarking data that have assisted Hills Road in knowing how well its performance compares with others. Value-added calculations, which compare actual A-level results with what General Certificate of Secondary Education results implied should happen, are already used in many schools and colleges. The recent notion of creating families of schools and colleges working in similar environments with similar intakes promises to make tables of raw results more meaningful. In a good college, governors, principal and staff will want to be aware of such data so that they can celebrate their successes and identify areas for development. At Hills Road, benchmarking has been applied to a range of performance indicators that assist in the process of identifying and promoting quality and achievement. The governors and staff receive an annual performance report which includes data relating to recruitment, attendance, course completion, achievement, added value, lesson observations, student satisfaction and destinations after leaving the college. The report plays an important part in the setting of challenging annual targets for the next year. In addition to whole-college benchmarking, each department creates an annual report according to a predetermined data template. Such reports are valuable complements to the whole-college picture and enable departments to identify strengths, weaknesses, trends, issues for further discussion, professional development needs and the degree of student satisfaction within a department. This latter is a key element. There is much to be gained from regular meetings of departmental staff with students. Similarly, in the whole-college context, a lively, democratically elected student council provides opportunities for student leadership and a valuable forum of communication between staff and the student body. Informing the use of all such performance data is a belief in the critical importance of self-assessment.

Quality appointments

Perhaps the single most important activity undertaken by the principal and senior colleagues is to appoint the right staff. If they are successful in this area, college and departmental annual reports are likely to make more satisfying reading. In the interests of students, appointments procedures deserve serious thought and planning. Moreover, colleges that do not use transparent and rigorous procedures, including carefully recorded notes, are increasingly at risk of litigation from unsuccessful candidates. At Hills Road, the selection process for teaching posts includes observing candidates working with a selection of those for whose learning the successful candidate may be responsible for many years. This process and a series of informal interviews occur in the morning, candidates having been warned that some may not proceed to formal interviews in the afternoon. While this degree of rigour is time-consuming, it has served Hills Road well, although it is recognised that in the present problematic state of teacher recruitment, some schools and colleges may not be fortunate enough to enjoy the competition for posts that such a model presumes.

Quality professional development, appraisal and performance management

Having appointed a new member of staff, as a good employer the college assumes a responsibility, shared with the successful candidate, for their professional development, beginning with a comprehensive programme of induction. At Hills Road, induction involves a series of presentations given by senior staff and middle managers, followed by opportunities for clarification and discussion. Induction also provides an opportunity to ensure that there is no ambiguity about professional expectations. It cannot be assumed that expectations are the same in all schools and colleges. When budgets are tight it is tempting to cut back on staff development, but this is invariably a mistake. Like the college of which they are a part, staff will not stand still: they either develop or ossify.

Formal appraisal systems are now well embedded in most colleges, but professional conversations alone are no longer an adequate means of ensuring good performance and professional development. Lesson observations, balanced statistical performance data and an appreciation of contributions to the general life of the college community also deserve consideration in pursuit of a well-rounded picture. This process is most fruitful if staff have agreed the scope and methodology of appraisal-related matters and are committed to whole-college, departmental and individual self-assessment processes. It is also important at the outset to establish that the purpose of appraisal and performance systems is to celebrate good practice as well as to identify areas for professional development. Staff with departmental responsibilities should expect to assume important roles in this process and staff development issues should feature prominently in the departmental annual report.

For senior staff in some colleges there has been a trend towards performance management pay. While such pay can be seen as a way of encouraging and rewarding effective and successful leadership, in a profession that places great store on collegiate values and in which leadership is essential at all levels, performance management pay can be divisive and damage the sense of partnership between senior and other staff that is the hallmark of a good college. If performance management pay is used by governors for some staff, it should not reduce resources available for other staff and it must be awarded against clear criteria agreed at the beginning of the period under review. In using systems of performance management pay, governors need to maintain a clear distinction between pay for performance, job weight and the annual cost-of-living review.

The appointment, professional development and motivation of able and well-qualified staff has played an important part in the response of Hills Road to the central challenge of creating a stimulating and vibrant learning environment. Although teachers and teaching must be the architects of such an environment, emphasis on learning is also crucial. The learning culture requires a genuine sense of partnership between teacher and student; availability of open-access library and departmental resource and study areas for staff and students; and easy access to high-quality ICT facilities throughout the college. An attractive, friendly and well-cared-for environment, in which carpets, curtains, paintings, sculptures, plants, flowers and grassed areas have a natural place, encourages the college's students and staff to feel good about their place of work.

Staff and students: expectations, involvement and support

Another vital ingredient is staff and student conduct. Within the basic framework of statutory requirements, staff and student handbooks that have been drawn up in consultation with those who are expected to observe their contents are essential if expectations are to be clearly understood and uncertainty avoided. When problems occur, it must also be clear who is expected to initiate discussions aimed at encouraging better conduct. Both staff and students are entitled to expect agreed procedures to be followed to the letter and to be offered support in overcoming any difficulties. It is important to make an accurate record of events for possible future reference.

In addition to unavoidable staff absence through sickness, it is essential to monitor and control the accumulation of days of staff absence for activities that are legitimate and valuable, such as professional development and extramural activities for students. Having encouraged its student body to be hungry for learning, the college whose staff are frequently absent, however legitimate the reason, will soon find disillusionment among students whose learning and pattern of work is regularly disrupted.

Even in the most successful and happy of colleges, from time to time staff will leave. They can, however, perform one last service, namely agreeing to participate in an exit interview. No longer having an axe to grind, they are a valuable source of commentary on the strengths and weaknesses of a college as perceived by a typical member of staff. At Hills Road, exit interviews are carried out by the senior member of staff responsible for staff development. Discretion, experienced evaluation and the occasional pinch of salt may be needed, but the outcomes will invariably be of considerable value.

While high-quality support and guidance for students of all ages is a vital part of student entitlement, teachers who are engaged in such work at the transition from Year 11 to Year 12 have particular challenges to which they must respond. Perhaps for the first time, students will be taking decisions that may have profound consequences on their lives. One such decision is between employment and continuing in education or training. For those who opt for the latter, choice of subject, course and institution can be difficult. Students are entitled to receive impartial guidance and to be provided with easy access to all the opportunities available to them. At Hills Road, more than 99 per cent of the 800 sixth form students who enrol each year are able to study the precise combination of subjects of their choice, a factor that undoubtedly has a beneficial effect on levels of student satisfaction, retention and achievement.

Assuming that the sixth form student has enrolled on the right course in the right institution, how should their support and guidance be arranged in an environment where they will expect more choice and freedom? A comprehensive induction programme at both college and departmental levels is essential. Students may well have taken into account values and expectations when making their choice of centre, but these need to be amplified on entry. Similarly, teaching and learning strategies and patterns of work are likely to be different from Year 11 and this needs explanation and discussion. Some students may find the first term of Year 12 unexpectedly stressful and disorienting, especially those whose studies require considerable open-mindedness because there are no right or wrong answers. All this reinforces the need for a personal tutor who knows the student well and will support them through initial difficulties. The professional development of such tutors is vital if they are to undertake their role effectively. They must not see this work as of lower value than teaching, to be fitted in when time allows. For a significant number of students, the quality of the support and guidance that they receive from their personal tutor, and from other staff, plays a vital role in their sense of identity, self-esteem, willingness to stay the course and ultimate success. The personal tutor is also central to a system of regular progress review, helping individual students to make coherent sense of subject teachers' contributions to the review. The personal tutor should also act as advocate and supporter in times of difficult relationships with other staff, while reserving the right to challenge as well as support their tutee as circumstances demand.

A valuable source of support for many sixth form students is the Study Skills Centre, where a range of learning difficulties can be addressed on an individual basis. Dyslexia, time-management problems, development of reading and essay-writing skills are some of the issues that may best be addressed with the help of a specialist in study skills. It is important that the Study Skills Centre is an attractive area and is given a prestigious location. The more students make use of the centre as a normal part of their learning environment, the more likely its work is to be valued by staff and students alike. At Hills Road, approximately 25 per cent of the student body use the Study Skills Centre.

Another specialist service that may be of particular benefit to sixth formers is the professionally qualified counsellor. At a time in their lives when relationships with home can be precarious and deeply sensitive issues may need to be addressed, the opportunity to talk in complete confidence with a professionally skilled adult can be of immense value. How such a service should be made available is debatable, as few schools or colleges can afford the kind of self-referral arrangements available in universities. Nor may self-referral be appropriate for the sixth form age group. Whatever the system of referral, it is essential that confidentiality between counsellor and student is maintained. It is also important that the selection of counsellors for the college's panel, whose work may best be undertaken off the premises, is as rigorous as the selection of the college's teaching and support staff.

Years 12 and 13 soon pass and students will once again be considering their options, but on a much wider canvas than in Year 11. They benefit greatly from impartial guidance as they consider the worldwide multitude of options available to them. Careers guidance agencies normally arrange fairs at which employers and institutions of higher education promote the opportunities on offer. Preparation in advance of the fair and opportunity for informed discussion afterwards are key aspects of guidance at this stage. At Hills Road, the Careers Department plays a vital role in this respect, including providing information about the destinations and experiences of previous generations of students. Former students are invited to talk about their experiences in employment, in higher education and in gap-year projects such as those promoted by the British Schools' Exploration Society, Operation Raleigh, Project Trust and Voluntary Service Overseas. At Hills Road, more than 30 per cent of students take a gap year, often using part of their time to work and travel in other continents. Parents, too, benefit from evenings when they can learn about the financial implications of higher education. Nor should the value of example be underestimated. Many students in Years 12 and 13 may wonder whether they can aspire to higher education. They will be encouraged to know that some of those who were recently in the same position have gone on successfully to university and are enjoying the experience.

Celebrating success

Part of the successful learning environment is the celebration of achievement by groups and individuals. In a large college, ensuring that every member of the community knows about other students' achievements is a considerable challenge but pays handsome dividends. Similarly, it is important to establish constructive links with the local media. In this way goodwill can be encouraged in the local community, which will help to place bad news – which inevitably occurs in the best of colleges from time to time – in a sensible perspective. Individual, group and team successes are a cause for public celebration, such as a certificate evening or prize giving. These take a great deal of staff time to organise and are worth doing only if the quality of the organisation reflects the importance of the occasion. Nevertheless, the inspiring words of a well-chosen guest of honour and the goodwill that reverberates in the local community are invaluable. At Hills Road, guests of honour at prize giving have included Rabbi Julia Neuberger and Lord Dearing, both of whom spoke with wisdom and humanity while being wonderfully appreciative of students' achievements.

All schools and colleges want their students to be proud of being a member of their community and only the most precociously cynical adolescent will deny the value of such celebrations. However good other promotional materials, undoubtedly a school's or college's own students, proud of their successes and pleased to be a member of a community where they have thrived and been valued, are best placed to sing praises. Schools and colleges whose students perform well should not hesitate to put them up front as often as possible as an example and an inspiration to present and future generations of students.

8

■ ■ ■

Why Bother with the Creative Arts in Schools?

by Dame Tamsyn Imison

I will never forget on a drab day driving through the wasted hinterland of Birmingham, noticing the unkempt verges, the tenement blocks and the burnt-out cars, and then arriving at a primary school, a low, prefabricated building with grilled windows. I came into a warm, rich, welcoming environment full of students' paintings, models and artefacts, where friends from the community had disguised the necessary iron cages round the computers as Aztec castles – cages were essential, as the last break-in had been carried out using a bulldozer straight through the breeze-block walls. The haven was Moat Farm Junior School and the lucky children, encouraged to be creative and challenged to learn well, had achieved well above the national average.

My own school, Hampstead School, in North London, looked very like the outside of Moat Farm when I arrived as a new head 16 years ago: dirty, graffiti-covered, and with nothing of the students except for a few self-portraits in the foyer that had been up so long that people had pinned notices over the faces. I used to spend two hours a night cleaning off graffiti and painting walls as well as photocopying good students' work which I put up on the walls. This work was not touched. My first 'present' to each department was a set of frames for them to mount students' work and put it up in their public areas. An excellent headteacher whom I had shadowed had done this to great effect in a tough London school.

How many of us have developed an aesthetic awareness of our surroundings and the messages such surroundings give out to all who live in them: messages about valuing students and their own work; messages about what quality work is; messages about beauty and indeed spirituality? Art departments are often beautiful places, but the opportunity for the students' work to make statements about valuing all students and about creating beauty and harmony is frequently missing across school. I had to wait more than ten years to get an outstanding head of art who commandeered every space as a natural foil for brilliant students' work which kept getting better and better. She also takes over a local art gallery to exhibit Advanced Level work, which for two years running was all of 'A' quality and recognised as such. What does external appreciation do for these students? All gained places in top art schools or added these skills to a broad portfolio for university entrance in a wide range of other areas.

This head of art also integrated life-drawing classes into the core curriculum, much to the admiration of Office for Standards in Education inspectors who were struck by the professional and mature attitude of the students. Artists in residence and visits to artists' workshops are built into the prescribed curriculum to give our students the opportunity to understand what it is like to make your living in this field. They also provided further examples of excellence, and the discipline and rigour needed to achieve well. The art department regularly takes students abroad to Barcelona, Paris, Venice and Florence. They all bring back sketchbooks packed with the most wonderful drawings, paintings, studies and ideas, which are works of art in their own right. These are on open exhibition in the art area and provide outstanding models for the younger students. Such visits are so enjoyable that other teachers fight to be included and as a result all participants have written poetry, composed music and experienced a holistic approach to learning. Examples of the work and poetry are on our school web page on www.hampsteadschool.org.uk.

Art is for all

Raymond Williams in his seminal work *The Long Revolution* (1961) links art with the development of communities. He says:

Art is the organisation of experience.

and

Human community grows by the discovery of common meanings, common means of communication. Over an active range, the patterns created by the brain and the patterns internalised by the community continually interact. The individual creative description is part of the general process which creates conventions and institutions, through which the meanings that are valued by the community are shared and made active.

As a head of year in Pimlico, a specialist music school, I saw for myself the danger of elitism, with other students not on the specialist course feeling rejected. In their turn they rejected music and also those students who were part of it. This polarisation was extremely dangerous. Once we involved the music students in playing rock and jazz as well as classics in our assemblies they became perceived very differently and the assemblies became so popular that students from other years regularly tried to get into them.

Sometimes in the past in my own school, I had a tough time persuading very talented students to participate in the girls' choir – the only whole-school group that the then head of music was able to manage. It was outstanding and won national awards, but the angst generated on all sides was a real turn-off and many students gave up doing music. We had very few concerts and I will never forget the first of these when a students' band was relegated to play in the interval while everyone except myself was out having a drink.

In complete contrast, my present music staff are determined that all students should enjoy, compose, play and develop a real appreciation of a vast range of music and use new technologies to support this. They too, like the art department, have moved out of their department and commandeer time and space for students to perform, listen to, and enjoy a wide range of their own and others' music. A creative link with Trinity College of Music has provided our instrumentalists with superb role models and opportunities to play alongside professionals as well as offering master classes for some of our gifted and talented pupils. The DJ classes and the soul group have brought in professionals from very different backgrounds who have also been able to foster and develop excellence in many students who were previously seriously under-motivated.

Costing the arts

The problem with music in schools is often the cost. Many parents now have to pay for their children to learn to play an instrument and often have to buy the instrument for them to play on. Students have to fit music rehearsals and practice into an already massively overcrowded timetable. All departments need resources and facilities in order to deliver, but effective use of these is essential. Often, peripatetic staff are undervalued and not brought in to be full members of the department. My present head of music has a whole-school plan fully involving all peripatetic staff who provide taster groups for Year 7 to try out instruments and, with the Local Education Authority, provide good opportunities for students to borrow instruments until they can purchase their own.

What we needed to do as our part of the development was to use money from hiring out school facilities to create a centralised department with an office, recording studio, two good music rooms, access to the hall, practice rooms and small group rooms, computers and keyboards and sufficient security. We are extremely fortunate to have an enterprising director of site and services management and development who was able to realise what the department needed by clever conversions of hallways, toilets and cupboards.

Concerts, chamber groups and a multitude of musical activities in and out of the curriculum are now a regular feature of school life, as well as the annual tour abroad to perform in places such as Strasbourg, Venice and New York. Recently I have not needed to coerce students into participating. Instead, I have been expected to, and enjoyed, attending every event. Participation is not just for students but all staff and parents as well as others in the community. Our last year's Christmas concert on CD is a favourite of mine, especially the brilliant rendering of part of *The Messiah*, in which everyone participated – students, staff and parents. There were wonderful solos from a past student who is now a music scholar at Magdalen College, Oxford, and a member of our science staff who is an impressive countertenor. This occasion was truly spiritually uplifting and the feeling of pride by everyone present was deeply moving.

For many years we had no school drama productions and the theatre and 'plays' were not in evidence. This changed with the appointment of a head of department who loved the theatre, and her productions were both imaginative and inspiring. Examination results soared. Her first production was a traditional mystery play acted out around the hall, with scaffolding towers used to maximum effect. The Chinese student playing Joseph and the Asian girl playing Mary had such tranquil dignity, while the robust humour of the strolling players and the dynamism of an outstanding Afro-Caribbean as 'God' contrasted brilliantly. There was a huge cast and an involved audience who could not bear it to end. It was a magical event and transformed everyone's expectations of drama in the school.

The same head of drama, discussing with the playwright David Edgar the need for good new plays by top writers for schools, followed up his suggestion of creating the National Schools Playwright Commissioning Group. This links up to 20 schools across the country that, in banding together, raise the £30 000 needed to commission a playwright and a composer to work with the students in the schools to produce a play with music. This is relevant to the children in these schools and ensures they can take a significant part in the process of writing and composing. David Edgar had come into our school to participate in an exciting sixth-form induction programme, *The History of Western Thought*, since modified and broadened to cater for more than 70 home languages from all over the world.

So far this national group, now firmly established, has commissioned twice: Adrian Mitchell wrote *The Siege* with music by Andrew Dickinson, and John McGrath wrote *On the Road to Mandalay* with music by Rick Lloyd of Flying Pickets' fame. This venture is unbelievably exciting and is the 'poor' school's way of having a top playwright in residence to produce a commercial work especially for them. Oberon Press published Adrian's play and we expect that

John's play will also be published and available to other schools after our world premieres in 2000 and 2001.

The students' perceptions of this commissioning have been positive but, most particularly, it has raised the status of the arts, provided students with an active, meaningful involvement in the creative process as well as providing us with a piece to perform that is tailor-made to the students. Neither play was easy or played down to the students. Instead, the students had to raise their standards to deliver to the high expectations of top professionals. Good reviews in the national press raised their esteem and status further. These experiences are on top of very full repertoires.

High profile and life skills

Drama provides opportunities for students and staff to acquire many essential life skills that will make the difference between career success and failure. Many people fail because they cannot relate to others and have not learned how to co-operate with, participate in and lead groups. Communication is visual as well as verbal and the 'hidden' signals we all send out, including the way we walk and 'own' the space, are often far more important. These also are essential for commanding the respect and interest of most students. One of our best professional development sessions was on this topic; good use of a staff meeting, delivered by our new head of drama to the whole staff. It was the talk of the staff room for some time and significantly changed practice because it was relevant and colleagues could see that it worked. This head of drama is an outstanding import from Derbyshire who knew of our school through the National Schools network.

Dance has similarly made a significant impact upon the whole school. We have been lucky to have had a succession of good heads of dance who have inspired a wide range of students from outstandingly gifted to those who have not been afraid to have a go, regardless of sex, shape or skill level. This area has also had more self-motivated students who have the opportunities in assemblies and other whole-school events to display their talents and enthusiasm – wonderful Asian dancers with exquisite hand and foot movement, Irish dancers, Croatians, as well as rap and rock dancers, which have changed staff and student perceptions and increased participation. School council evaluations of assemblies showed how much they valued the whole-school assemblies with student participation as an integral part.

Often, stunningly talented teachers are like the 'cats that walk on their own'. By having whole-school productions with an emphasis on co-operation, music, dance, drama, art and design have become aware of the value of cross-curricular support and involvement. All other teams are also then keen to assist with the important facets of success: publicity, front of house, refreshments and, most important, active appreciation shown by attending and praising all concerned.

Acceptable risk taking

A young and talented design technology teacher, who is also a musician and passionately interested in the theatre (where he had worked before coming into teaching), asked me whether he could organise a whole-school, whole-day creative arts celebration. Always keen to encourage young talent, my immediate response was 'yes'. It was a huge undertaking, but we found some money to support the venture. However, disbanding the curriculum even for one day and allowing 1300 students and 120 staff freedom to select a range of creative options, some outside in the community, was pretty scary and there were moments when we seriously wondered whether we should cancel the event. In the end, with strong senior support, the expected day arrived and it was wonderfully warm and sunny.

It remains in my mind as a high spot because, given autonomy, both staff and students were wonderful. The staff offered a huge range of activities, which they personally enjoyed, and participated in them alongside the students. The artists in residence added an extra dimension, but it was the imagination and creativity of both teachers and students that was particularly impressive. The sixth-form common room, where the director of post-16 had links with people in the Notting Hill Carnival, was taken over as a design and making studio, creating bright, showy and unique costumes which were later much appreciated in the local community Jester festival (even though it poured with rain). Another room was transformed into a peaceful haven by removing all desks and chairs, clothing the whole area – ceilings, walls and windows – with lining paper and then cutting windows to see a vase of scented flowers, a collection of natural objects with water bubbling through, and spirals of twisted lining paper suspended from the ceiling. In here other staff practised Mongolian chanting with some of the students.

Outside, some of our Asian girls were painting wonderful henna designs on willing students and an admiring queue formed. Over in a grassy area an enthusiastic geography department was encouraging teams of students to build the best shantytown and there were hammers, nails, ladders, wood – but no mishaps – and the 'houses' created were greatly appreciated by everyone. Along the road a graffiti-covered shop and wall were getting a face-lift by a boy in Year 10 to a design that had been chosen by members of the community. The work done then survived being torched by some miscreants, and still looks great today.

In the hall, students were creating a huge wind instrument out of vast, brightly coloured piping. This was work with an amazing artist-musician in residence. A music technology workshop was hard at it in a year room led by sixth-form students. Skills were learned and music was created all day. Next door, students and staff were making lovely things out of brightly coloured paper for an exhibition later in the day. A group of students wrote and performed a

Victorian melodrama around the school. Others wrote poems produced in a magazine. In the science labs, students and enthusiastic staff transformed a dismal pre-war lab into a luxuriant tropical rain forest. These were just a fraction of the activities. The real plus was the meaningful sustained industry and enjoyment, the lack of disruption, the completion of each task to the satisfaction of all, no damage or injury, and a sense of real achievement and appreciation of others. The only group who missed out were the parents, who heard how exciting it was and wanted to join in.

It would have been easy to use the overcrowded curriculum as an excuse for not holding such an event. We would all have been the poorer. A primary colleague, now retired, said he could no longer use opportunities such as appreciating a wonderful rainbow, because he had to deliver the literacy hour. Surely the opportunity provided for motivating and stimulating both teachers and students – by unforeseen happenings such as a rainbow, or built-in happenings such as our creative arts celebration – are worth all the effort and ingenuity as well as being acceptable risk taking. Sometimes we create boundaries and barriers to learning and use external requirements as excuses.

We need to realise the true value of the creative arts as a motivator, stimulator and as the means to achievement for many youngsters whose preferred learning styles mean they learn best by active participation.

In my previous school, Abbey Wood in South East London, I saw some miracle transformations through drama – students playing in Molière suddenly getting a taste for literature and going on to university as first-generation entrants from a school where the aspirations of the majority were far more modest. It was in this school that I organised three large whole-community events for nearly 2000 children, using more than 200 students as organisers alongside me. This was sound sense as the staff were not used to undertaking anything outside their classrooms. The first event was a book event we called a 'Book Bang'. The second was a science fair we called a 'Whiz Bang' and the third was a creative arts symposium. They were cross-phase events involving the lower school at our secondary, comprehensive, secondary modern and 13 feeder primary schools. One outcome that delighted me was the increase, by one-and-a-half forms, of entry in our previously falling roll school.

These events were truly cross curricular and involved suspending the curriculum for a whole day, but they also involved lots of preparatory work for all those who took part. Each group who came met two practitioners and took part in some practical and creative events as well as looking at a huge public exhibition, where all the students had work on show, and visiting two bookshops on the school site. The named contributors who came included Leon Garfield, Roald Dahl, Marjorie Darke, Quentin Blake and Patrick Moore, among many others. We had more than 40 top names for each event because it was the individual students who approached the writer, scientist or artist. It is hard to say 'no' to a child. Reading through the evaluations, all of which were very positive, it was clear that the group who gained the most were the students who had helped me with the organisation. Many formed personal links with professionals, some of which exist to this day.

One of the other outcomes was a dramatic improvement in the secondary display, as I had cannily suggested primary colleagues mounted their work first. In primary work it is quite natural to produce illustrated responses to work crossing all curricular divides. This comes less easily to specialist graduates, but they rose to the occasion. Examination results also improved in subsequent years for those who participated. An enjoyable section of the exhibition was a wall of portraits showing students' perceptions of what their writers, artists or scientists looked like. This was fascinating for our visitors, who took it all in good part.

The last of our events, the creative arts symposium, will always be linked for me with a visit I made to the deprived home of one of our youngsters, with a front room housing a dirty couch and a television set, closed curtains and a wreath of cigarette smoke. I had come to bring the girl a present from the artists she had looked after. Both artists were well into their seventies and made exquisite marquetry pictures. They had been so impressed with the care they had received that had made the girl a beautiful picture. She was ill when they brought it in, so I was delivering it. She was so thrilled that tears filled her eyes and she asked me what she should give them. I told her she had already given them a present with her care and thoughtfulness, making sure they knew where to go, getting them tea, taking them to lunch and looking after them for the whole day. In her evaluation, like so many others, she said that taking responsibility for others was what she had valued most about the whole event. The acquisition of such personal skills is vitally important.

These are all examples from my experience, and my commitment to strong, active, participatory creative arts underpinning every school is based on this. I think I have made it clear that I have a broad view of the creative arts. I am looking at the full range I have mentioned above, including English, but I am also describing an intermeshing of delivery so that other areas give purpose to the arts while the arts support and enhance them. In short, what is essential is a broad, balanced curriculum delivered by mutually supportive teams of specialists. If this can be achieved, the motivation of staff and students is greatly enhanced because they are within a creative learning environment where the ethos is such that creative approaches are considered to be acceptable and people are supported to use occasional failures to move even further forward.

Arts in the curriculum

If, as I have suggested, the arts specifically and collectively have a profoundly positive impact on the whole-school ethos, learning environment and classroom delivery, how do you appoint, keep and develop good teachers in the arts? I believe firmly in modelling and the power of the mirror effect. Teachers and students will gravitate towards where things are exciting and fun, where they are well supported, but most particularly where there is learning and experimentation. Creativity is a facet of good, effective learning and the creative arts satisfy many subconscious needs, such as a beautiful learning environment and the opportunity to have fun with others and to work to some purpose collectively. We have found that selecting and retaining good staff is dependent on these things. We have also used students to assist in the selection process by evaluating applicants who have been short-listed, as every person applying has to teach a group of students. Involving students has proved to be very positive and has prevented the selection of those who have mugged up on the right interview answers but do not have the skills to work well in a team or with staff. We are always looking for those who will gain further promotion, as we would rather have an excellent short contribution than a long deteriorating one.

You might argue that by delivering drama through English and dance through physical education, you save yourself the expense of separate specialists and curriculum time. We have done this for dance, but it puts huge stresses on the teacher responsible for dance and it is not nearly as satisfactory as separate specialists. Status is important for each area of the curriculum because this is known to influence students' selection of subjects in Key Stages 4 and 5.

What about curriculum time? We have just moved to a ten-day cycle in order to free up time and to remove disastrous carousels, which bedevil much creative arts delivery in Key Stage 3. This is the period when most students experience turn-off and it is vital to have a vibrant, exciting curriculum, which supports students through the worst of adolescence and negative peer pressure. This is where a strong creative arts programme will support student motivation and encourage them to try out more challenging learning.

I would strongly recommend that you read the summary of the National Foundation for Educational Research (NFER) report published in 2000, *Arts Education in Secondary Schools: Effects and Effectiveness*. I hope that my experience exemplified here illustrates all the main points made in this important report. It also shows how these issues come round again as there are many similarities with the important but forgotten report produced by the Calouste Gulbenkian Foundation (1989). The NFER report identifies the nine most influential factors that contribute to effective learning and teaching in the arts:

- the status of the arts;
- adequate provision for the arts at Key Stages 3 and 4;
- the enjoyment and perceived relevance of the arts;
- internal and external support for the arts;
- specialist teachers;

- practical task-based activities;
- performance, display, evaluation and symbolic celebration of what is produced;
- a praise culture;
- pupils' own contribution, background and parental support.

The learning outcomes for pupils observed in the study are:

- a heightened sense of enjoyment, excitement, fulfilment and therapeutic release of tensions;
- an increase in the knowledge and skills associated with particular art forms;
- enhanced knowledge of social and cultural issues;
- the development of creativity and thinking skills;
- the enrichment of communication and expressive skills;
- advances in personal and social development;
- effects that transfer to other contexts, such as learning in other subjects, the world of work, and cultural activities outside of and beyond the school.

The outcomes identified for the school are:

- institutional effects on the culture of the school;
- effects on the local community, including parents and governors;
- art itself.

Footnote

Please do not be misled by the name Hampstead School. We should be called Cricklewood High. The school is situated adjacent to the main railway line in the far northern corner of Camden, between Cricklewood Broadway and the Finchley Road. If you step out of the school and walk north you are immediately in Barnet; the other side of the track is Brent. Fifty-three per cent of our students come from outside Camden, the majority from Brent. The housing is a real mix, with three large council estates; late Victorian and Edwardian property, some with multiple occupation and others gentrified; as well as bed and breakfast accommodation. On the boundary of our catchment area, now just under 1.5 kilometres in radius, is Hampstead Garden Suburb. Opposite the school, replacing prefabs, is a 'new', 1993 estate being used to house disadvantaged families.

The multi-ethnic nature of the school arises from a complex population, with a well-established, more traditional 'village' group, small enclaves of minority communities who retain their customs and practices, as well as a more varied mix of people who have relatively recently found refuge through the local borough's supportive policy towards asylum seekers. We have more than 100 students in this category, nearly one-third of whom arrived as unaccompanied minors. Seventy per cent of the school roll (just 20 per cent in 1985) is made up of ethnic minorities. Eighteen per cent of these are at stages 1 and 2 of assessment for special educational needs (SEN). Students in the school speak more than 70 different languages .

Our percentage of girls to boys is 46:54 – not as significant as in the other mixed schools where only about one-third are girls to two-thirds boys. We have targeted parents with prospective girls, recognising that with 23 more forms of entry for girls than boys in Camden this would always be a key issue. We have traditionally taken students from more than 50 feeder primary schools, but this number has now dropped to 40 as the school has become more popular and the catchment area has reduced. Thirty-three per cent of our intake are entitled to free school meals and 36 per cent have single parent status. There are 60 statemented students (ten in the sixth form) and 472 other pupils are on the SEN register at stages 2–4.

References

Calouste Gulbenkian Foundation (1989) *The Arts in Schools* (led by Professor Ken Robinson).

National Foundation for Educational Research (2000) *Arts Education in Secondary Schools: Effects and Effectiveness.* Summary and commentary.

Rogers, R. (1998) *The Disappearing Arts? The current state of the arts in initial teacher training and professional development.* London: RSA.

Williams, R. (1961) *The Long Revolution.* London: Penguin Books.

9

■ ■ ■

Arts in Schools

by Malcolm Noble

The excellency of every art is its intensity, capable of making all disagreeables evaporate, from their being in close relationship with beauty and truth.

(John Keats, 1817)

Arts are undervalued in the National Curriculum, yet they are not so in our economy, nor in our national heritage. The 1999 report *All Our Futures: Creativity, culture and education* places arts education within a context of creativity and culture. The report's definitions are a good starting point. Creativity is seen as 'imaginative activity fashioned so as to produce outcomes that are both original and of value', while culture is defined as 'the shared values and patterns of behaviour that characterise different social groups and cultures'. *All Our Futures* envisages creative and cultural education as extending across the curriculum. The arts must, however, be central.

They are far from central to the National Curriculum (1997). Only art and music are foundation subjects. The Arts subjects now have just one attainment target divided into level descriptions. Art and music have their own programmes of study. The emphasis on skills is important to creativity; that on appreciation provides access to culture. However, no arts at all need to be followed after Key Stage 3. The Secondary Heads Association (SHA) saw the importance of drama to creativity in 1998. 'Adaptability, team working, empathy and team working' were all seen as being enhanced by good drama teaching at all key stages.

The National Curriculum is strongly based on subject specialism, an approach that has been challenged by the Royal Society of Arts (RSA) which advocates a learning framework based on *competencies* (Bayliss, 1998a). The National Curriculum 'would be built around new *competencies*; it would continue in broad terms the subject coverage in schools'. Subject specialisms would stay.

Nevertheless, the RSA sees more change in schools as a result of the 're-engineering' it proposes, 'than any other part of the system'.

It is the opportunities created by the new technologies that are driving much of the debate on schools for the 21st century. The RSA claims schools have not exploited the 'vast potential of broadcasting in the digital age'. The government also sees it this way. In 1997 it wanted schools linked to a National Grid for Learning (NGfL), providing modern teaching and resource materials linked to the internet by 2002. In *Towards the Classroom of the Future* (2000) the Department for Education and Employment (DfEE) envisages new technologies as giving 'all students their own home page and creating links between schools, local communities and the world at large'. The London Grid for Learning (NGfL 2000) will provide a network linking schools across all London boroughs. This is a high-speed computer network operating from the autumn of 2001, which will provide schools with access to information from a range of providers, including broadcasters, museums, galleries and the 33 member local authorities themselves.

Creativity and culture

The two strands of creativity and culture provide the framework for this chapter. The new technologies connect with cultural education. The NGfL, for example, will 'foster links with galleries, business and community organisations'. Education for creativity, however, depends on the interaction between teacher and learner. *All Our Futures* suggests that 'creative processes require both the freedom to experiment and the use of skills, knowledge and understanding'. Fostering those uses is the duty imposed upon teachers by the Education Reform Act 1988. Teaching for creativity may be a less straightforward proposition. Anyone imposing their creative ideas on young people is unlikely to encourage independent thought or initiative. This is difficult for teachers trained to drive pupils through programmes of study, towards the promised land of examination success.

A paper written for Arthur Andersen Business Consulting (Walker, 1998) on the globalisation of education tackles this problem. The author acknowledges the danger that information and communications technology (ICT) could take us even further in the direction of 'consumer-driven packaged education'. To combat this the paper suggests that 'the effective educator must have the time and flexibility to play the role of facilitator rather than the constant expert'. Teachers should 'develop effective ways of making self-directed learning flourish in a virtual environment'.

Teachers of arts subjects are well placed to develop creativity. Many have feared that the arts would not have a secure future in schools, but the SHA found that in 1995 provision in Key Stage 3 appeared to be strengthening, though concerns remained for Key Stage 4. A paper delivered to the Vision 2020 Conference in 2000 looked forward to an enhanced professional status for teachers. Its authors believe:

> *The best teachers will be able to sell their services to many learning communities around the globe, either directly or digitally. There will be a group of highly paid, respected expert teachers and presenters who will have a worldwide profile.*

They want a creative curriculum taking up 30 per cent of the timetable and focusing on 'process skills such as thinking, analysing, problem solving and team working'.

In 1997 David Blunkett, Secretary of State for Education and Employment, told the Technology Colleges Trust:

> *The child who cannot read cannot learn; the child who cannot learn cannot flourish in the creative world of the new century.*

This heralded the Labour government's drive to improve basic skills. It also acknowledged the importance of creativity. Today ICT is counted as a basic skill. ICT is capable of playing a decisive role in the development of creativity. Lack of investment in hardware, software and training of teachers will hold back progress for a while.

IT leads the way

Information technology has immense potential in enabling the arts to contribute to creativity in schools. Specialist packages for computer-aided design, computer-aided manufacture for art and music, and lighting for drama, all support the individual arts subjects. Planning school productions can benefit from the use of generic software for word processing and the use of spreadsheets. Accessing information through multimedia can enable pupils to consider a range of options for any project and the best format for presentation. This is a view of information technology as a tool for the learner. It gives the learner choices simply not feasible with face-to-face teaching styles, thus enabling pupils to produce work more competently and presenting opportunities for more individual creativity.

It is, however, communications technology that now offers opportunities that will define the difference between the first years of the new century and the last years of the old one. New communications systems place control in the hands of the individual learner. E-mail and e-mail attachments are highly efficient as a means of communication, and are also entirely in the control of each individual. Pupils need to be taught how to plan and present messages, but once they have mastered the basics, ready interchange of information is not bounded by classroom or school, nor even by country.

The internet provides an obvious access to culture. The teacher can facilitate routes into information and help evaluate the quality of content. Visiting museums' and galleries' websites allows pupils to follow their interests. Many school websites are promotional devices, seldom visited by the children. Websites can be used for files on educational projects, celebration of pupil achievements, reminders on dates and deadlines, and advice for parents. Used in this way, the web pages can also make homework more of a creative endeavour.

The RSA (Bayliss, 1998b) advises teachers that if they are to lead people forward, they 'must visibly be part of the new world rather than the old'. Using interactive whiteboards, for example, is a powerful statement of commitment to new technologies. It also gets children used to handling information in a variety of media at the same time.

It is, however, the use of video-conferencing that holds the greatest promise for extending the cultural reach for young people. However, it isn't easy to find other users. Setting up links, especially overseas, remains a difficult and time-consuming task. Teachers have to worry over such considerations as getting the lighting right and developing a sense of timing that would do credit to a professional actor.

Digital broadcasting and home-produced videos permit learning that is not bound by time and place. Video-conferencing, however, enables groups of children in different places to work together, to see each other and talk to each other. By setting up projects between schools in different countries, both can enhance their knowledge and understanding of different cultures. The arts have to take the lead in using this medium. Visual and performing arts are at the heart of all cultures and most people are happy to share it with others. Finding ways of using video-conferencing requires ingenuity from all concerned and positively demands creativity.

The emphasis on the virtual curriculum is not going to save the government any money. If teaching and learning in the arts are to be modernised, then a great deal must be spent on providing the right facilities. High-quality facilities should foster high standards of work. This might, however, be achieved through community links. Specialist spaces for individual arts subjects tend to meet only the requirement of subject specialisms. The arts-centre approach can combine performance and exhibition spaces with shared areas, including ICT networks. These can then be a resource for the local community. They can also raise the profile of arts in both school and community.

The restrictions imposed by the National Curriculum do not prevent pupils having access to the arts at Key Stage 4, and given the flexibility now available it is no longer difficult for children to opt for two arts subjects. Extra-curricular activities allow children to take advantage of performance and exhibition spaces. This can still mean, however, that children can opt out of the arts curriculum altogether.

Celebration of the arts

The arts festival is a means of ensuring that everyone benefits from the contribution of the arts, in respect of access to culture and the development of creativity. Roger McGough OBE, the poet, inaugurated the first Bexleyheath School Arts Festival in 1996. Two weeks in July are given over to arts-based activities in this mixed, 11–19 school on the outer edge of London.

There are three strands. The first is internal, with departments contributing arts-related activities within their subject specialisms. This includes the production, which is the climax of the festival and was *Carmina Burana* in 2000. There are many cross-curricular projects. A joint languages and art project takes place in the South of France and focuses on the work of the artist Cézanne. The food technology and language departments run a French café throughout the fortnight. The science department sets out a new garden on the school site.

The second strand involves access to professionals, either within school or at theatres, museums and galleries. Music has been represented by the Japanese Taiko drummers and the London Adventist Chorale. There have been many dance companies, including the IRIE African-Caribbean group and the Cholmondeleys (all male) and Featherstonehaughs (all female). Individual authors, poets and actors have included Eric Richard (Sergeant Cryer of *The Bill*), Jennifer Stoute (Rebel from *Gladiators*), The Reverend Roly Bain (the church's jester), Patience Agdabi (poet) and Jean Ure, James Sale, Peter Beere and Roy Apps (all writers). The Globe Players and the BT-sponsored National Theatre performance *Sparkleshark* have been festival highlights.

The third strand is the community profile. The festival is funded largely by business sponsorship and the efforts of the parents' association. There is involvement from the police, town centre business and local organisations, but there is scope for a lot more. Daily events are, however, posted on the school website, primarily for the benefit of parents. A glossy brochure, sponsored by the local council, aims to involve parents and raise the profile generally. It is also intended to impress the sponsors.

The essence of an arts festival is that everyone is working intensively for a time on a common endeavour. It is a difficult thing to do. Schools revolve around routines and are driven by timetables; an arts festival can be expensive and place strains on the school's administration. However, arts festivals are arranged to fit the particular circumstances of an individual school and can provide a model for education in the 21st century.

The arts festival can provide access to cultural education and develop creativity. The model has four elements:

- arts festival;
- teaching and learning;
- culture;
- creativity.

The first consists of the content and the activities that take place during the festival. It connects access to the culture of this and other nations. This involves access to professional performance and exhibitions. Virtual access is fostered through digital broadcasting media, multimedia and the internet. Teaching and learning represent the contribution made by departments, through specialism or in a cross-curricular way. These should be skills based, often delivered through workshops and creative processes.

There are infinite possibilities for the way an arts festival is organised in any school. If the arts festival is simply an 'activities week', designed to keep everyone busy at the end of the year, it cannot contribute much to cultural and creative education. If it is to have a significant and long-lasting impact, then the following might be applied in almost any situation.

Planning

The arts festival should form part of the development plan for the school and individual departments. These must be linked to the aims of the festival. There should also be explicit objectives for the contribution of each department or group within the school. Central planning is necessary for budgets, community involvement, booking professional participants and outside visits, workshops involving primary schools, and general co-ordination. One approach is to collapse all normal activities and prepare a timetable for the duration with, perhaps, the tutor group as the basic organisational unit.

The staff concerned must employ project management skills. Objectives should be divided into tasks monitored at pre-set milestones. If project budgeting and scheduling are to be manageable at all, this must be a computerised operation. If the work for the arts festival begins and ends within a fortnight, there are unlikely to be long-term benefits. Schemes of work must prepare children for the arts festival and lead to follow-up work after it.

Learning

A 'one size fits all' approach will negate everything a school is trying to achieve through an arts festival. Creativity will be fostered only if the opportunity is there to follow individual interests. Equally, not everyone will appreciate cultural opportunities in the same way. Giving pupils a free choice from what is available might not be manageable. It may not even be desirable. Children may be inclined to stick with what they know and can do. Creativity should involve challenge and a willingness to experiment.

A way of squaring the circle is to have experiences that must be followed by all groups. Instead of relating these to the individual arts, they might be expressed as types of activity. These might be *appreciative, performing, workshop* and *community*. Viewing an exhibition or attending a play would be *appreciative. Performing* could be anything from playing instruments, singing, participating in sports to holding a principal part in the school production. This can prove the most difficult area for older children. *Workshop* has a practical basis, with some kind of definite output. *Community* can also present practical difficulties – work experience or community activities undertaken throughout the year might be counted as meeting this objective.

Portfolio

The model requires a focus on culture and creativity for individual children and groups. It might be possible to set tests at the end of it all, although some teachers might consider there is quite enough testing in the system already. If, alternatively, all the children were set an individual project, which would include a requirement to evaluate the activities relevant to them, the outcome could be an important contribution to their record of achievement.

The project is the opportunity to ensure that all children use ICT during the arts festival. By utilising the internet or e-mail, or visiting websites, pupils can gather information on their own account. They might then use a variety of software packages to give a presentation on what they have achieved in a personal, computer-based portfolio.

Evaluation

It could be argued that pupils and their parents will not take the arts festival seriously unless it relates to the examination system or is certificated in some way. If this century does see testing of competences replacing traditional examinations, this is likely to be a problem. Schools may, therefore, consider use of prizes and certificates based on the pupil portfolio. An alternative is to have the whole operation quality assured by external consultants, then have an externally marked or moderated system for the pupil portfolio, allowing a standard to be set for graded certification. This would cost even more money, however.

Missing from this model is explicit reference to an international dimension. The use of video-conferencing here is what can really set this apart from past practice. Workshops involving arts-related activities crossing cultures and continents should be central to an international arts festival. Visits and exchanges normally involve a small minority; everyone can participate in video-conferencing link-ups. This may not be possible during the festival itself, but some of it might happen during the planning stage.

The starting point

The model outlined above requires a strong arts presence as a starting point. If the arts are based in a modern centre, with shared performance and exhibition space, plus ICT capability, so much the better. The model views the arts as the means whereby young people gain access to culture and develop creativity. Cultural and creative education are not in any sense limited to the arts. The idea is that all departments can work with arts specialists to realise the aims of the arts festival. They need to look at their work schemes and decide what is most appropriate for this purpose. The school must also consider the contribution of the spiritual, moral and social elements of the curriculum, and now presumably citizenship.

This is not an alternative to examination courses in the arts. The arts festival is about access for everyone, while allowing individuals and groups some leeway to pursue their own interests. The justifications are that culture should be available to all and that creative ability is essential for most careers. Hopefully, though, the performance aspect may give encouragement to those wishing to follow courses in music, drama, art and the rest to Advanced Level and into higher education. In fact, the arts are taking their place alongside languages, mathematics, the sciences, technology and the humanities as required areas of study.

The application of new technologies is essential for planning and presentation. Communication facilities dramatically extend the range of what is possible. The knowledge, skills and understanding that pupils gain through the arts are increasingly seen as having equal value. Sustaining the arts for all children after the age of 14 helps to maintain breadth and balance in the curriculum. The arts festival model can be adapted for all abilities and a range of interests.

An international arts festival, underpinned by ICT, including video-conferencing, can achieve much for all schools. Specialist institutions might just have bigger and better festivals. They will be even better if schools have modern arts centres. It can, however, take years to build up the necessary expertise in arts-based project management and an adequate level of sponsorship. Pilot schemes supported by the government or the Arts Council might provide a suitable starting point.

A project management template for arts festivals could be devised and tried out in pilot schools. There is, of course, a problem with the title. There are arts festivals and arts festivals! A week of fun activities and a musical production might be graced with the title. An arts festival that is rooted in the curriculum and focuses on pupil achievement is a different kind of enterprise altogether. Unlike the other sort, it cannot be static. If there is no regular innovation, there is unlikely to be much in the way of access to culture or development of creativity. This is one example where external help can make a difference. Assisting schools with innovative approaches of this nature is essential if as complex a model as this is to be tested and improved to the point where it can deliver value for money.

There is certainly a wind behind the arts in Britain. Lottery money and the millennium have provided the impetus. There is much support for the view that creative skills are necessary for work in the new century. Schools must seize the moment to secure funding and access to training, first of all for teachers to improve their ICT skills. Schools have to innovate in the arts, as with any other sector, if they are to benefit from the favourable climate.

Business sponsorship is crucial to the arts in Britain. Summer arts festivals depend on regular sources of sponsorship, hence different levels of 'friends' groups. A justification for promoting arts education is the benefits it confers on young people in working life. A determined attempt to involve local communities, and especially business, in arts education in schools could be facilitated by the Arts Council, local arts councils and the Department of Culture, Media and Sport. Help with premises improvement and use, perhaps through sponsoring, productions and renting spaces, would be a valuable contribution.

Nevertheless, there is a danger in over-emphasising academic rigour in the arts. Young people might also be persuaded to recognise, with Keats, the place of 'beauty and truth'.

References

Bayliss, V. (1998a) *Redefining Work*. Report reference 4 on competencies in the curriculum. Royal Society of Arts.

Bayliss, V. (1998b) *Redefining Schooling – A challenge to a closed society*. Discussion paper reference 6 on using interactive whiteboards. RSA.

Bexleyheath School (1999, 2000) Arts Festival brochures.

Blunkett, D. (1997) 'Raising educational standards and improving work skills for the 21st century'. Speech to the Technology Colleges Trust.

DfEE (1997) *Excellence in Schools*. Report reference 5 on National Grid For Learning. White Paper.

DfEE (2000) *Towards the Classroom of the Future*. Report reference 6 on the use of new technology.

HMSO (1988) Education Report Act Section 1.

HMSO (1997) *Connecting the Learning Society*. The National Grid For Learning consultation paper, reference 8 on the purpose of the National Grid.

National Advisory Committee on Creative and Cultural Education. (1999) *All Our Futures: Creativity, culture and education*. DfEE.

The National Curriculum (1997 version) DfEE.

National Grid for Learning (2000) *London Grid for Learning*. Booklet reference 7 on London Computer Network. Website www.lgfl.net

Secondary Heads Association (1995) *Whither the Arts?*

Secondary Heads Association (1998) *Drama Sets You Free.*

V2020 Executive Group (2000) 'One world one school' Vision 2020 conference paper, reference on a curriculum for the 21st century.

Walker, G. (1998) 'The globalisation of education' for Arthur Andersen Business Consulting.

10

■ ■ ■

Literature and Emotional Intelligence

by Keith Cox

Hipperholme and Lightcliffe High School is a mixed 11–18 comprehensive foundation school of 1000 students in East Calderdale. Calderdale itself is split into three divisions. East and West Calderdale have comprehensive secondary schools, while Central Calderdale, based on the town of Halifax, retains a selective system, with two foundation grammar schools.

Hipperholme and Lightcliffe is a popular and oversubscribed school, whose catchment area has changed in recent years. Recruitment has come increasingly from the school's designated feeder schools rather than from across the whole district of Calderdale. Although the school is situated in an area of Calderdale with one of the highest indicators of potential educational advantage, its areas of actual recruitment include those with the highest indicators of potential educational disadvantage. It is, therefore, felt to be a genuinely comprehensive school, albeit with the two selective schools having an effect upon recruitment at the top of the academic ability range.

It is an interesting point as to what constitutes the official voice of a school.
(Riley, 1998)

It is most definitely much more than the voice of its assistant headteacher. Although the 'change' which I wish to describe owes much to the insights that I have gained at Hipperholme and Lightcliffe High School, it is also the product of working with a number of other agencies, schools, teachers and individuals.

Nowadays, the National Curriculum makes radical curriculum innovation difficult, especially at Key Stage 3. The literacy and numeracy strategies, imposing as they do not merely the subject matter but also the methodology of teaching, look set to impose even tighter constraints:

> *The real message schools have been given is that they should pose no serious questions for their curriculum to answer, but should concentrate on administering an imposed system.*
>
> *(Ungoed-Thomas, 1997)*

Surely teachers should have a vision of education that drives their work?

An educational journey

As a classicist by training, my interest in language and literature is longstanding. However, it was through the professional freedom given to me by my headteacher that I had the opportunity to work with a number of colleagues to create a humanities curriculum from first principles, drawing on the work done by HMI on the Entitlement Curriculum. Richard Pring was also an influence on our work. At a time when personal and social education was in danger of being equated with a narrow concept of 'lifeskills', he saw personal and social development at the very heart of all teaching and within the values that permeate a school (Pring, 1984: 168–169).

The National Curriculum quickly convinced me that education is much more than a collection of subjects and I found myself in charge of literacy and numeracy, cross-curricular themes, and personal, health and social education (PHSE). Fate then brought me responsibility for the Technical and Vocational Education Initiative (TVEI) and taught me much about teaching and learning styles, relevance and the vocational curriculum. It was through TVEI that I pursued my interest in the use of information and communications technology (ICT) to aid learning. In recent years staff development and how we invest in people have become dominant interests. Total Quality Management, re-engineering and the structures and leadership styles of industry have shaped my ideas on both leadership in schools and the education that we should provide for our students.

In my own teaching, I come back to language and literature, even more convinced of its value. What has given a theoretical base to my ideas and experience is the work of Howard Gardner on multiple intelligence and of Salovey, Mayer, Goleman and others on emotional intelligence.

Background and theory

For as far back as people have been writing, the power of literature has been recognised instinctively. Plato chose to exclude poets from his republic, not because they served no purpose but because he was concerned that their influence would not suit his objectives. Aristotle recognised the role of literature in exploring the human condition:

> *Poetry is something more philosophical and more worthy of serious attention than history; for while poetry is concerned with universal truths, history treats of particular facts.*
>
> *(Aristotle, Poetics: Ch. 9)*

Over the past 15 years we have begun to learn how the brain works. We are beginning to understand why literature has such an important role to play in the development of our brains and our learning. If we remind ourselves of how the brain actually functions, it is the middle section, the limbic system, that controls our emotional response. However, our emotional response is much more than a list of emotions. The limbic system controls our memory, our self-image and values, and has a major influence upon our decision-making process:

- In times of extreme stress, we lose control. LeDoux has shown that there are circuits in the limbic system that bypass our slower, rational thoughts and provoke an immediate emotional flood (Goleman, 1995) – the 'flight or fight' response of our primitive ancestry. Goleman calls these 'neural hijackings'.
- Working memory is stored in the prefrontal cortex. Strong emotional signals from the limbic system to the prefrontal lobes – anxiety, anger, a sense of injustice, loss of status – can disrupt this memory to the point where our thinking is impaired. We simply cannot concentrate. Little wonder that there is such concern at the high levels of stress being recorded in the teaching profession (*Times Educational Supplement*, December 2000).
- Decision making at its most effective is a partnership between the limbic system and the neo-cortex (the section of the brain that deals with rational and creative thought). We store our emotional experiences in the limbic system and the brain uses these (sometimes subconsciously) as part of the decision-making process.
- Our self-image, contained within the limbic system, is one of the most powerful factors in its impact upon our performance and success.

It was Salovey and Mayer, two American psychologists, who first formulated the theory of emotional intelligence. In 1997, Salovey (Salovey and Sluyter, 1997) revised this thinking and defined emotional intelligence as comprising four components:

1 *Emotional facilitation of thinking* – a recognition of the role that our emotions play in thinking and decision making.
2 *Reflective regulation of emotions to promote emotional and intellectual growth* – the way we manage emotions in ourselves and others.

3 *Understanding and analysing emotions; employing emotional knowledge* – describing and labelling emotions.

4 *Perception, appraisal and expression of emotion* – ability to identify and recognise emotions, both real and false, in ourselves and others.

Daniel Goleman has developed the ideas and applied them to the world of work (1998). He describes the ideas differently but covers similar ground:

1 *Self-awareness* – understanding your emotions and their impact, strengths and weaknesses, sense of self-worth.

2 *Self-management* – self-control, trustworthiness, conscientiousness, adaptability, achievement orientation, initiative.

3 *Social awareness* – empathy, awareness of organisations, ability to recognise and meet needs.

4 *Social skill* – visionary leadership, influence, developing others, communication, change catalyst, conflict management, building bonds, teamwork and collaboration.

It is important to realise that emotional intelligence is not a soft option with no place in the real world. Recent work on leadership by consultants Hay McBer has identified six styles of leadership from a sample of 3871 executives chosen at random from its database of 20 000 worldwide. The first two styles have been found to have a negative impact:

- coercive style – induces fear, stress and resentment and encourages secrecy;
- pace-setting style – sets unreasonable demands, stifles initiative and produces stress;
- authoritative style – has a clear purpose and direction, people feel valued;
- affiliative style – focuses on people, loyalty and relationships;
- democratic style – values contributions and seeks out the best ideas, but can leave a group feeling leaderless;
- coaching style – takes a longer-term approach and builds on people's strengths, having much in common with the Investors in People approach.

Goleman (2000) has looked at the emotional competencies that underlie these styles. Little wonder that the government and Office for Standards in Education (Ofsted) approach has been so resented, relying as it has on the coercive and pace-setting styles – the two counter-productive approaches. It is also interesting to note that too much emphasis on 'challenge' rather than 'support' from local education authorities across the country risks putting school improvement in the hands of the emotionally inept. On the positive side, it would appear that empathy plays a major role in our performance as leaders and as members of a team, being a key competence in the three most effective styles: authoritative, affiliative and coaching.

If emotional intelligence is so important to our performance and success, how do we ensure that our curriculum develops emotional intelligence in our students?

Theory into practice

Current themes in classics at Hipperholme and Lightcliffe High School include leadership and multiple intelligence; anger as an obstacle to success and co-operation with others; self-respect; the search for revenge; the power of love; duty; self-interest and corruption in public life.

It can be argued that through the teaching of classical literature it has been possible to help students to develop an understanding of their emotions and to empathise with the situations and feelings of others. It is possible that this experience helps to control our own emotional floods and improves the quality of our thinking and problem solving. The study of complex ideas and the development of characters gives time for what Claxton (1997) calls slow thinking, when the brain is able to process difficult problems that have no clear answer, or no answer at all. It allows us to make links with previous experience and learning and we know from research that the brain actually learns through the formation of links.

The study of literature helps us to build a richer store of memories and reference points which help our thought and decision making in the future. Our memory is improved if we attach emotional experience to our learning. If the atmosphere of the classroom is right, we can achieve that state of relaxed alertness that is most conducive to learning.

How can we test our success? General Certificate of Secondary Education (GCSE) Classics results in August 2000 were 17 points above the school's average for A*–C grades, but that is a meaningless statistic reserved for league tables. I suspect that the measures for success in emotional development are more complex. Csikszentmihalyi (1997) talks of 'flow' as the measure of success, by which he means that mental state in which time passes very quickly, something significant has been achieved and the experience has been enjoyed.

The problem we face as educators in the current climate is that things that cannot be tested as fast thinking and measured on a performance table are pushed aside in favour of those things that can. Tests involving fast thinking take place under pressure (usually time pressure); they usually require students to work alone; they often deal with problems outside students' experience; the types of questions are those that have a clear right answer.

I am proud when my students receive their examination certificates, but I am really proud when a student has enjoyed the exchange of complex ideas with a group of fellow students and says at the end of a two-year A-level course, 'You have given me an insight (which could be described as being a passion) which has grown and I am sure will continue to grow throughout my life'. Learning sounds strange and unfamiliar when it is expressed from our emotional mind. It is not easy to make league tables out of comments of this kind.

Implications and issues

Unfortunately, there is evidence at Key Stage 3 (KS3) that the study of literature is under threat.

Let us start with a simple issue. The KS3 dip. Answer? Continuation of the literacy strategy into KS3. The response? Organise in-service training, send the English department to observe Year 6 lessons in the local pyramid, buy some large textbooks and set a date for the writing of medium-term plans – the 'delivering the curriculum' approach.

Research on leadership suggests that leaders have the confidence to ask some uncomfortable questions (Gardner, 1995). What KS3 dip? On which criteria? Where do puberty and adolescence fit in all this? Why do middle-class students gain in scores over the summer while lower-class students have lower scores (Sainsbury et al., 1998)? Why do most countries experience a 'dip' at this age? To be fair to the Department for Education and Employment (DfEE), research has been commissioned and some searching questions are being asked, including questions on the nature of learning and the culture of schools (DfEE, 2000a).

Are we so convinced of the all-embracing success of the literacy strategy that we are prepared to see it taking the place of 'English' at KS3? Take booster classes, the government's programme to give additional support for Year 6 classes in order to make the literacy and numeracy strategies more effective. According to the DfEE, the programme has been made more flexible in response to teachers' ideas. Anne-Marie Binns from Griffin Primary School, Kingston Upon Hull, talking about her out-of-school booster classes, says:

> We were able to get to know the children better and have a better relationship with them. A sense of humour comes out with them as they are now relaxed, and I am more relaxed. The children tend to come out with all sorts of ideas.
>
> (Teachers, *April 2000*)

The article goes on to say:

> Teachers have seen an increase in children's confidence levels across the board and parents have even reported improvements in their child's behaviour at home.

Ruth Green's comments (ibid.) point to the importance of a secure environment:

> They are not sitting quietly at the back not listening. They want to do the best they can and improve. It's important that we raise their self-esteem and motivate them so they can do it.

Do these comments not raise some serious questions about the primary school's curriculum and culture of care (Prosser, 1999) if these issues are not being addressed in the literacy hours themselves? As Hugh Busher points out in his preface to Jon Prosser's book:

> *Pupils are among the actors within a school who help to shape its culture. They are not merely passive baskets to be filled with bread neatly wrapped in National Curriculum packages.*

As we have seen above, literature has been recognised from Aristotle to the present day as one of the most effective ways of supporting emotional development. The draft *Framework for Teaching English Years 7–9* sees literature as a vehicle to deliver a set of linguistic objectives:

> *In planning to deliver the range of texts required by the National Curriculum, teachers will choose and use texts to deliver the objectives. In this way, pupils in one school studying, for example,* Treasure Island *and* Animal Farm, *will, one way or another, have covered the same objectives by the end of the key stage as pupils in another school who have studied quite different texts.*

> *(DfEE, 2000b)*

Could it be that emotional development is not a mere by-product of number 13 of the text level objectives for reading, or of booster classes, but one of the key facets of intelligence that underpin all learning?

Leaders of learning should have the confidence to draw upon and adapt the ideas and experience of others. There have been many initiatives, observations and research projects that have recognised the importance of emotional intelligence in the crucial middle years of education, including a number of PHSE initiatives in Britain. As our students make the transition to secondary education, many factors are affecting their development.

Puberty/adolescence

> *There is a biological clock inside us that begins the process on which education has little influence.*

> *(Solodow, 1999)*

The changes that occur through puberty and adolescence put the literacy strategy into perspective. New hormones, emotions, physical change, neurons in the brain changing the quality of thought towards abstract reasoning – in other words, new ways of thinking, feeling and behaving – have a significant influence.

Particularly important is the changing perception of relationships. Peers take on a much greater importance in terms of values and allegiance. Some young people experience a strong feeling of rejection and develop a very negative self-image. Appearance takes on major importance, giving rise to emotional storms ('Why isn't my blouse ironed?' 'You haven't *washed* my trousers, have you?'). The key characteristics are self-preoccupation and self-esteem:

The fear of making mistakes and looking foolish is one of the strongest obstacles to developing high self-esteem and motivation. Students with a positive self-image view mistakes as experiences to learn from while those with low self-esteem perceive mistakes as failures that cannot be corrected easily. The latter group of students are likely to retreat from school tasks that they believe will lead to further failure and frustration. I believe that minimising the fear of mistakes is one of the most important challenges faced by educators.

(Brooks, 1999)

Young people begin to question the adults, parents and teachers whom they used to put on a pedestal. In their tastes they rebel against adults, establishing their own identity through music and fashion. In terms of learning, they become less interested in correct answers and more able to focus on the learning process. This is also true of emotional and moral development, where there can be a variety of causes and circumstances to explain behaviour and feelings, the beginning of the notion of empathy. Quality time for reflection needs to be provided at this crucial stage of development:

Without reflection, social and emotional learning remains fragmented and temporary at best.

(Charney et al., 1999)

As a paradox, emerging adults need to check and validate their emerging roles, values and images. Here schools and the sort of classrooms we set up can play a key role:

At a time when many middle school youngsters ruminate about themselves, their negative self-perceptions often convince them that they are not smart, not liked, or not attractive. A responsive classroom curriculum provides these young people with opportunities to express and explore their concerns ... The daily life of the classroom becomes a safe community in which adolescent issues can be shared among peers and in which students can be guided by a caring adult.

(Patti and Lantieri, 1999)

We cannot stop puberty, but we can influence the values that emerge through adolescence and affect people's emotional development for the rest of their lives:

Educators must realise that they have a major impact on students, not just concerning what occurs on a particular day but for the rest of the students' lives. We must move away from the simplistic view that teaching academic skills and content is separate from promoting the growth of a student's emotional and social well-being. Focusing on the whole child does not detract from teaching academic material. Rather both domains are parts of the same fabric and are inextricably interwoven. If any part of the fabric is weakened, the entire fabric may unravel; if all the fibres are strong, the total fabric will be resilient.

(Brooks, 1999)

What is it that people remember from school? A well-placed semi-colon, or feeling humiliated by a well-intentioned but emotionally illiterate teacher maintaining pace at all costs:

> *Academic grades and SAT scores are extraordinarily nonpredictive of satisfaction and productivity throughout life. Emotional well-being, on the other hand, is dramatically and positively predictive not only of academic achievement but also of satisfactory and productive experiences in the worlds of work and marriage – in fact, it even is predictive of better physical health.*
>
> *(Cohen, 1999)*

School leaders need to develop a curriculum and culture that ensures that cognitive and emotional development work in harmony. As Terri Apter explains in the book for parents that she subtitles 'Raising children to believe in themselves':

> *Psychologists now realise just how important emotional intelligence is: an emotional education is every bit as important for life skills as an intellectual one. As we explain why we sometimes feel as we do, and behave as we would rather not, we offer our children perspectives on the adult world. We forge a link between their knowledge of what it is to be themselves – in their child's world – and their perception of the world into which they are maturing.*
>
> *(Apter, 1998)*

Changing schools

At the point of transfer to secondary school, students' reference points and security are suddenly removed, yet this reference point is crucial to their ability to learn:

> *Unless students feel part of a community, unless they feel motivated to work, struggle, master, they will never be able to benefit from formal education.*
>
> *(Howard Gardner, in the foreward to Cohen, 1999)*

At a time when adolescents are re-examining their roles with adults, they lose contact with the well-established and comfortable ties of one teacher and are faced with a variety of new teachers, and new peers:

> *We must recognise that students will learn most effectively in an atmosphere in which they feel safe and do not fear being ridiculed or humiliated, in which they are challenged and assisted to meet realistic goals, in which they feel teachers genuinely care about them and respect their individuality, and in which learning is seen as an exciting adventure rather than drudgery.*
>
> *(Brooks, 1999)*

Brooks goes on to cite belonging and feeling connected, feeling autonomous and having a sense of self-determination, and feeling competent as the features of a nurturing environment.

The demands of learning change just as students' ability to use abstract reasoning develops. The curriculum needs to recognise and make use of these changes:

> For the first time, the student sees that many interpretations of data are possible and that a particular course of events is but one of many possible alternatives.
>
> (Solodow, 1999)

If only our political leaders could reach this stage of development! Learning in the secondary school needs to be different.

> Adolescents often have concerns involving personal space, furniture, display of student work, time constraints and the need for physical activity in a classroom environment.
>
> (Charney, et al., 1999)

Again, transfer takes its toll in terms of loss of security. Remember, the natural reaction of the brain to stress is 'fight or flight'.

For adults, too

Emotional intelligence is not an example of what Chris Woodhead described as a 'distraction of pseudo-academic obfuscation' (*Times Education Supplement*, January 2000). The loss of self-image caused by an Ofsted criticism for lack of pace can and has destroyed the life of a dedicated and experienced teacher. Through emotional intelligence, and particularly empathy, teachers are better able to work effectively with students, colleagues and parents.

In the business world, research by the Drucker Foundation to inform work on the leader of the future discovers that the leaders of the top-performing organisations derive their power from:

> ... the dignity they nurture in those around them and at all levels in their respective organisations. ... Their power lies in their ability to foster relationships.
>
> (Heskett and Schlesinger, 1996)

Stephen Covey (1996) defines the roles of the leader as pathfinding, aligning, empowering. He sees a major shift in the value base of leadership:

> The leader of the future will be a leader in every area of life, especially family life. The enormous needs and opportunities in society call for a great responsibility toward service. There is no place where this spirit of service can be cultivated like

the home. The spirit of the home, and also of the school, is that they prepare young people to go forth and serve. People are supposed to serve. Life is a mission, not a career. The whole spirit of this philosophy should pervade our society. I also think that it is a source of happiness, because you don't get happiness directly. It only comes as a byproduct of service. You can get pleasure directly, but it is fleeting.

According to Kouzes and Pozner (1995):

Traditional management teaches that leaders ought to be cool, aloof, and analytical; they ought to separate emotion from work. Yet when real-life leaders discuss what they're the proudest of in their own careers, they describe feelings of inspiration, passion, elation, intensity, challenge, caring, and kindness – and yes, even love.

We need time to reflect, and to 'know ourselves', an expression as effective now as it was in the days when it adorned the shrine of Apollo in Delphi:

This awareness of emotions is the fundamental emotional competence on which others, such as emotional self-control, build.

(Goleman, 1995)

What better medium than literature to help us with the task.

References

Apter, T. (1998) *The Confident Child: Raising children to believe in themselves*. New York: Bantam Books.

Aristotle, Horace, Longinus (1965) *Classical Literary Criticism*. London: Penguin Books.

Brooks, R. (1999) 'Creating a positive school climate' in *Educating Minds and Hearts: Social emotional learning and the passage into adolescence*. Columbia University: Teachers College Press.

Charney, R., Crawford, L. and Wood, C. (1999) 'The development of responsibility in early adolescence' in *Educating Minds and Hearts: Social emotional learning and the passage into adolescence*. Columbia University: Teachers College Press.

Claxton, G. (1997) *Hare Brain, Tortoise Mind*. London: Fourth Estate.

Cohen, J. (1999) 'Social and emotional learning past and present' in *Educating Minds and Hearts: Social emotional learning and the passage into adolescence*. Columbia University: Teachers College Press.

Covey, S. (1996) 'Three roles of the leader in the new paradigm' in *The Leader of the Future*. San Francisco: Jossey-Bass

Csikszentmihalyi, M. (1997) *Finding Flow – The Psychology of Engagement With Everyday Life*. New York: Basic Books.

DfEE (2000a) 'Give them an extra boost' in *Teachers*, Number 8, April.

DfEE (2000b) *Framework for Teaching English Years 7–9*. Draft.

Gardner, H. (1983) *Frames of Mind: The theory of multiple intelligences*. New York: Basic Books.

Gardner, H. (1995) *Leading Minds*. New York: Basic Books.

Gardner, H. (1999) *Intelligence Reframed*. New York: Basic Books.

Goleman, D. (1995) *Emotional Intelligence*. New York: Bantam Books.

Goleman, D. (1998) *Working with Emotional Intelligence*. New York: Bantam Books.

Goleman, D. (2000), 'Leadership that gets results' in *Harvard Business Review*, March–April.

Heskett, J. and Schlesinger, L. (1996) 'Leaders who shape and keep performance-related culture,' in *The Leader of the Future*. San Francisco: Jossey-Bass.

Kouzes, J. and Pozner, B. (1995) *The Leadership Challenge*. San Francisco: Jossey-Bass.

Patti, J. and Lantieri, L. (1999) 'Waging peace in our schools' in *Educating Minds and Hearts: Social emotional learning and the passage into adolescence*. Columbia University: Teachers College Press.

Pring, R. (1984) *Personal and Social Education in the Curriculum*. London: Hodder and Stoughton.

Prosser, J. (1999) *School Culture*. London: Paul Chapman Publishing.

Riley, K. (1998) *Whose School Is It Anyway*. London: RoutledgeFalmer.

Sainsbury, M., Whetton, C., Mason, K. and Schagen, I. (1998) 'Fallback in attainment on transfer at age 11: evidence from the Summer Literacy Schools evaluation' in *NFER Educational Research*, vol. 40 (1).

Solodow, W. (1999) 'The meaning of development in middle school' in *Educating Minds and Hearts: Social emotional learning and the passage into adolescence*. Columbia University: Teachers College Press.

Salovey, P. and Sluyter, D. (1997) *Emotional Development and Emotional Intelligence – Educational Implications*. New York: Basic Books.

Ungoed-Thomas, J. (1997) *Vision of a School: The good school in the good society*. London: Cassell.

11
■ ■ ■

Social Inclusion in an Inner-city Comprehensive School

Is there an equitable model and provision for the inclusion agenda?

by Mo Laycock

We need to move further and faster in the inner cities. We need to tackle the problems of failure and low aspirations in the cities more directly, and we need a sharp, early improvement in parental confidence in the capacity of city schools to cater for ambitious and high-achieving students.

(DfEE, 1999)

No one involved in education would disagree with this statement. I applaud the government's vision, drive and tenacity to help support inner-city schools in creative and innovative ways. Since 1997 we have certainly seen in inner-city areas a greater understanding of the challenges for schools in such areas and a better balance of support versus pressure than in the previous 18 years. Inner-city schools were branded as bad schools, due to their league table position, with no understanding of the complex problems of urban communities exacerbated by unemployment, lack of hope, negative parental attitudes towards education (often based on their own educational failure), parochial attitudes, family breakdowns and poor council housing. The Excellence in Cities programme, increased Standards Fund resources, and focus on school improvement and self-review are all initiatives meant to pervade the educational system at all levels, with greater support for inner-city schools.

Inclusion is an area on which the government is firmly focused. Again I applaud this intention. My argument is that inclusion means different things in different schools and communities, and that this remains an inequitable model which, despite the extra recent and welcome resources, continues to make life more challenging in inner-city schools, and that inclusion, in particular, needs to be unpicked and examined in the context of the government's intention and policies if we are ever to move to a more equitable education provision for all school-age young people:

> Excellence in Cities *is intended to forge a step-change in tackling the particular problems of the major cities.*
>
> *(DfEE, 1999)*

Firth Park Community College, Sheffield

Firth Park is an inner-city school with 1300 pupils on its roll. It is an 11–16 comprehensive situated in Brightside, to the north-east of Sheffield. Of our 1300 students, the following indicators pertain:

- 48 per cent are on free school meals;
- 50 per cent are on the special educational needs register for learning and/or behaviour/emotional problems;
- we have a 35 per cent ethnic minority catchment, mostly Asian, African-Caribbean, Somali and dual-heritage students;
- as Sheffield offers refuge to asylum seekers, there are increasing numbers of pupils from Kosovo.

For those of you who have seen *The Full Monty*, the last scene was filmed in our local Shiregreen Working Men's Club! This is our claim to fame. Historically, the area was proud of its workforce, mostly steelworkers and manual/craft workers. Our catchment is almost entirely council housing and some of our local estates have high crime figures, areas of drug abuse, poor housing, a feeling of beleaguerment in living on these estates, and community members who do not feel that they live in Sheffield but in Shiregreen, which is somehow not part of Sheffield. Unemployment and single parenting statistics are high, as are the statistics relating to poor health and mental or emotional problems. Over the past 10–15 years the socio-economic position of the local community has deteriorated considerably, as has the morale of the area.

In September 1995, when I became the headteacher of Firth Park, the school had gone into the 'Serious Weaknesses' Ofsted category with the following indicators:

- teaching at satisfactory or better: 62 per cent;
- whole-school attendance: 77 per cent;
- three failing curriculum areas;
- poor systems and structures;
- unsatisfactory student behaviour;
- poor financial management and an inherited deficit budget.

The school also functioned across two sites, 2.4 kilometres apart, where students were bussed two or three times daily to access specialist curriculum provision and staff also had to travel. Firth Park became a comprehensive school in 1969, amalgamating Firth Park Boys Grammar School (the Brushes building) and Hatfield House Secondary School (the Fircroft building). I still have the letter from the then chief education officer who in 1969 promised to put Firth Park on to one school site within three or four years. Some 31 years later, in September 2000, this was finally the case, when we moved to the new and refurbished buildings on the Fircroft site and finally became one school team.

It was apparent to me in 1995 that the school had considerable potential, with a generally excellent and committed staff and warm-spirited youngsters. The school did, however, need to be led and managed in a different way, as identified in the 1995 Ofsted report.

By 1997 and a further inspection we had come out of Serious Weaknesses with the following indicators:

- teaching at satisfactory or above: 92 per cent;
- whole school attendance: 84 per cent (currently 86 per cent);
- no failing or weak curriculum areas;
- student behaviour generally satisfactory;
- strong leadership and management;
- sound financial systems;
- effective systems and strategies for further development.

The report stated 'Firth Park School is a rapidly improving school with all systems and structures in place for further improvements'. While the report left us with a big agenda of ten key issues and some clear challenges, nevertheless this was our first big step towards success.

Since 1995 we have increased student roll numbers to 1300 (65 below our accommodation limit). We have increased the budget provision through base funding and numbers on roll as well as such measures as Education Action Zone (EAZ) resources, Excellence in Cities (EiC), business sponsorship and New Opportunities Funding. We have also dealt with weak teaching through whole school quality assurance and monitoring arrangements and support and training of staff, as well as the use of formal procedures. Of the 78 teaching staff, 32 have been appointed since 1995, including a large proportion of bright-eyed and bushy-tailed young staff who, with other colleagues, have helped us to work in a positive school culture of high expectations and aspirations.

Yet we are still a school deemed to necessitate 'additional support' as we continue to function below national norms for 5+ A*–C General Certificate of Education (GCSE) results (2000: 18 per cent) and below 90 per cent whole-school attendance. As such the LEA/DfEE spotlight is still firmly focused on our school. We hope and believe that now we are finally a one-school site with more consistent communications, policies and procedures, we will finally get above 20 per cent at 5+ A*–C results in 2001. Yet there is speculation that this benchmark will move in 2001 to 25 per cent and we will continue to be a school necessitating this 'additional support'.

Student turbulence as a factor

As we also have a 20 per cent student turbulence statistic, particularly in Key Stage 4 where we have spare places, this situation is one of considerable concern. Like all schools, we set GCSE targets at the beginning of Year 10 based on Key Stage 3 SATs results and other school-generated data. These targets are aspirational but realistic and we are extremely creative in our efforts to help support and monitor students throughout the school. Yet in our Year 11 cohort of 2000, a year group of 220 students, after setting targets in 1998 we received, indeed *were instructed to take*, 23 extra students into Years 10 and 11. It is nationally known that movement into schools at Key Stage 4, with previous educational problems and the baggage accompanying these turbulent students, is unlikely to produce 5+ A*–C candidates. In fact, none of these 23 students had this potential. Many were damaged youngsters as a result of family or previous schooling issues. In June 1998 we also had four refugee students with no English joining Year 9. Add these issues to some 10–15 students who were either complete non-attenders or were on the work-related curriculum programme and not entered for any examinations, and one can see how the school failed to meet its 25 per cent 5+ A*–C target set in 1998. Having analysed these results and taken out the turbulent student figures, our results in 2000 were in fact 23.6 per cent at 5+ A*–C GCSEs.

Student turbulence is a real issue in many inner-city schools, and I believe that this needs to be taken account of in school statistics and improvement strategies, yet Ofsted has recently stated that turbulence makes no difference to school standards. I would strongly oppose this view in relation to critical mass issues and large numbers of students who consistently underachieve, feel that mainstream school is an alien culture, have complex personal, family and learning difficulties, and are more interested in their community credibility than success in educational terms. Having large numbers of these disengaged and often challenging students does affect school life on a daily basis and also the efforts and creativity of staff to support and try to motivate them.

As a consequence of the Excellence in Cities programme, increased Standards Funding and Student Retention Grant, for example, Firth Park Community College obtained considerable extra resources in the financial year 2000–2001. These extra resources were most welcome and through creative use of such funding, across cost centres, we were able to progress our school priorities and development planning in a much more strategic and positive manner than ever before.

Due to the additional funding we have received we:

- gained three learning mentors, all of whom are excellent;
- became lead school within a group of three in the Gifted and Talented strategy, again an excellent and most creative project;
- received extra funding for study skills, residentials, and extra-curricular opportunities;
- obtained a much increased Student Retention Grant;
- became a spoke school to a City Learning Centre, one of six spoke schools, with extra ICT resources;
- will have a Learning Support Unit (LSU) on site from September 2001.

It was agreed that LSU provisions across the secondary sector were to be placed in the nine Sheffield secondary inner-city schools. Sadly, our building project did not plan for this resource at the outset, so although we are the largest secondary inner city school in Sheffield, this provision will be in place at Firth Park 18 months later than in other similar benchmark schools.

Does the social inclusion agenda lead in practice to social exclusion?

All of these extra funds and strategies are being well used in our school, as endorsed by external personnel, but my enduring challenge is concerned with these questions:

- How do these extra resources and strategies enhance the attainment and aspirations of our student cohort?
- How does the local community interpret these extra resources for my college? Does this reinforce the notion that as a 'poor' school we need extra help?

- Does the LEA assume that we can therefore cater for even more troubled students as a consequence of these resources?
- What are the issues for my co-operative and hardworking students, as against a backcloth of a large number of disengaged and troubled students? Do these positive young people get a fair share of staff time, monitoring and encouragement or do the critical-mass issues weaken this provision?
- Is inclusion only a significant feature in inner-city schools?

It is my view that, unless we are very careful in the distribution of such extra resources and strategies, it could be assumed that inclusion resources are generally directed at the lowest achieving and invariably inner-city schools, so that we mop up together all or most of the challenging students within the secondary sector while other more middle-of-the-road, advantaged schools continue as normal. I would suggest that this could be the position LEAs and other schools are taking and that if this is the case, inner-city schools like Firth Park will continue *ad infinitum* to have major difficulties in climbing out of the 'additional support' and other harmful categorisations relating to national norms.

Where does the responsibility for more equitable inclusion lie?

At the secondary school level in urban areas, all secondary headteachers, their staff and governors across the city should ideally share the inclusion agenda. We should also share troubled and disengaged youngsters in a more equitable way. All of these youngsters have problems, but they also have potential, for which we should all share the responsibility. These young people deserve city-wide recognition and support if they are ever to resolve their problems and develop into active and responsible citizens. To place the majority of such youngsters in a limited number of schools is not fair to them, their potential, or indeed to the group of schools with critical-mass issues. Current legislation in relation to parental choice of school places means in reality that certain more 'popular' and 'successful' schools will always be full and unable to support more challenging and turbulent students. Other less 'popular' and 'successful' schools will bear the brunt of this difficult cohort.

As well as schools being full, other schools are in the Special Measures, Serious Weaknesses or Fresh Start categorisation and therefore not asked or instructed to take such youngsters. This reality is alive and well in Sheffield, where in 1999–2000 three secondary schools, including Firth Park, took the full force of permanently excluded, turbulent students as others were full or categorised as being in Special Measures. The effect on these three schools was considerable and this trend continues. All three schools are inner-city schools, with existing critical mass, 'additional support' issues. It does not take one long to work out how damaging ultimately this might be for these schools, for their continued development, or indeed being given an Ofsted or DfEE negative categorisation. I believe that all secondary headteachers, governing bodies and the local LEA share the responsibility of this possibility and that to ignore it is 'inclusion' only for certain schools and not a holistic, creative response to the problem.

Parental choice exacerbates the problem

The right of parental choice will continue to be legally enforced, as this means votes in any election. This is a particular issue in some parts of the country where the government naturally wishes to remain popular with the electorate. However, with this comes a self-fulfilling prophecy – those schools that do well in league table terms attract further aspirant pupils; those that do not are left with spare capacity and critical-mass issues.

With the willingness, shared ownership and responsibility for all school-age youngsters across all schools, we could engage in a more equitable model of inclusion and turbulence. Some areas of the country have engaged in this work, for example Kirklees in West Yorkshire, but perhaps the marked contrasts in socio-economic terms are not as pronounced in these areas as in others.

Yet if we could accept some shared responsibilities across all secondary schools, we could also perhaps share the problems and potential, and through networking learn from one another in relation to effective inclusion strategies. In so doing, current legislation would need to be altered and standard numbers in all schools considered in terms of school size and capacity. We could all agree to retain a proportion of places in each year group, dependent on school size – perhaps two or three per year group for a school of 700, four or five for a school of 900+, and six or seven for larger schools. In Sheffield, across 27 secondary schools, this would free up 126 places across the authority per year group. This sharing would be manageable. No school would have a disproportionate number of troubled, disengaged or excluded students and critical-mass issues, including negative attitudes to school, would reduce considerably.

Clearly this is a simplistic model and one that would necessitate further analysis. It also assumes that such youngsters are willing to travel across cities for their educational provision and furthermore there is an inherent assumption that the ethos and culture of the identified school is conducive to supporting such pupils. However, the latter is also a shared responsibility. If, in Sheffield, such a strategy was agreed to, we would potentially be able to support 630 secondary-aged difficult but potentially successful students together. This is real inclusion and not beyond the bounds of possibility. All schools, as a consequence of this sharing and equal responsibility, would also be allowed to engage these students proactively with the improvement agenda, and the playing field in relation to school success features would become more even.

Social inclusion and refugee-status students

Sheffield, along with other urban communities, offers refuge to asylum seekers, giving homes and security to families involved in civil war. Again this is laudable, yet the reality of this strategy is that families move to Sheffield, are housed in spare council housing, quite often without any community support in relation to their culture or beliefs, and their children are enrolled in local schools. Once again, these schools tend to be those with spare places and the most challenging situations.

At Firth Park we have currently 105 Somali students, all of whom are without exception wonderful young people. All are keen and aspirant, with warm personalities. Yet they arrive in Sheffield from a war-torn country, with no English, and often in extremely difficult family circumstances because of their experiences in Somalia. They feel they are in an alien culture, many have never had any formal education, and without any real support they are expected to fit into a school of 1300 students. More recently we have taken on to our roll ten students from Kosovo, again with no English or formal education. Five or six weeks before, these young people were given guns to shoot the enemy; now they are expected to adapt immediately to an inner-city school. There is no Albanian language support in Sheffield, nor is there a transitory safe house to help such refugees adapt to a new country and systems. This being so, we have to negotiate half-day timetables for such youngsters and a gradual integration into our school in order to support them and avoid shell-shock issues.

These students are also accounted for in our league table position at Key Stage 4, unless they join the school in Year 10, where they can be discounted from GCSE results. At Firth Park in 1998 we took in five Somali students in the June of Year 9, with no English. These students are now involved in post-16 courses and are doing well, but none of them attained 5+ A–C/A–G results, not surprisingly, given their circumstances. Yet if they had enrolled at Firth Park in the autumn term of 1998, their results could have been removed from our league table data. I have yet to see the research that states that a school can attain A–C/A–G results from refugee, non-English speaking students in seven school terms but not in six school terms. This aspect of turbulence seems to me to be a complete nonsense by the DfEE.

Furthermore, one of our Somali students, who arrived in Sheffield and at Firth Park in her Year 8 in 1996 with no English, achieved in 2000 an A in drama, A in art, B in expressive arts, C in English and four grade D results. In my opinion this is a great accolade for her and for Firth Park School's teaching and learning expertise, yet these results do not help our league table position.

Both of my sons went to secondary schools with reading ages of 15+ and attained excellent A*–C GCSE grades, but their formative years were very different to those of the Somali student's and up to a point their results were a self-fulfilling prophecy. This was not so in the case of the girl, who between

1994 and 1996 had witnessed considerable civil war issues in Somalia, had a gun shot wound to her neck, was in a most distressed state when she joined us, yet attained quite excellent results at GCSE level. She has now embarked on a post-16 A-level/General National Vocational Qualification (GNVQ) course at Sheffield College and I feel sure that in good time she will be a real success as she is a most determined and able young lady.

Planning for inclusion at Firth Park Community College

The current government strategy to provide schools with the resources to appoint adults other than teachers to support education in and outside of the school is, in my opinion, an excellent and successful development.

We are using our extra Standards Funding and EiC and EAZ resources to appoint the following personnel to join our valued support staff:

- a fourth learning mentor;
- a 50 per cent appointment of a college nurse to offer:
  - help and advice to students on health-related matters, including mental/emotional health issues, sex education advice, hygiene advice and general health-related issues;
  - support in relation to Personal Health and Social Education (PHSE) lessons and health-related matters, bringing into college external partners with an expertise in specific health areas;
  - a service tracking developments in first aid for staff;
  - the normal college nurse duties, such as vaccination;
  - links with parents for targeted students illustrating health problems;
  - workshops for parents on health and education-related issues.

Six of our 12 lunchtime helpers have been appointed as college and community workers. They have been appointed on a 20-hours-per-week contract to undertake the following:

- support at the break-time tuck shop;
- work with students with specific learning needs, helping them with reading and supporting them in lessons – we will provide training in this area and encourage these personnel to attain National Vocational Qualifications (NVQ);
- support in our 'Time Out', in-house exclusion base;
- co-ordination of lunchtime activities, i.e. 'Who wants to be a millionaire?' quiz workshops, and oversight of the video room/games rooms – these roles will complement existing lunchtime activities including ICT workshops, art workshops, dance provision, Learning Resource Centre activities and mathematics workshops;

- mentoring of Year 10 and 11 students along with other members of the support staff on a fortnightly basis;
- lunchtime duties;
- a 'sweep' of personnel at the end of lunchtime ensuring all students are in lessons;
- help with the lates' register and detentions system.

The appointment of our own educational social worker, contracted to Firth Park Community College, will co-ordinate the work and activities of our existing LEA-supported Education Welfare Service Officers (EWSOs). However, this appointment will be focused solely on Firth Park Community College and will target students with 75–85 per cent attendance, where we believe we can make a significant difference. EWSO personnel in Sheffield target pupils with 75 per cent and below attendance figures. We believe we need a more focused approach to the 75–85 per cent cohort, including rigorous work with students and parents. As such we would hope to see our attendance figures improve considerably.

In the USA schools in challenging areas all have a school counsellor to work alongside school staff and to provide confidential support to troubled youngsters. We believe that our students need this support, as many of their problems are complex and not focused solely on educational issues. We appointed a school counsellor in April 2001.

Through Objective 1 resources (European Social Fund) for South Yorkshire from April 2001, all secondary schools will have the resources to appoint a further assistant headteacher. At Firth Park this post will be focused on drawing together the inclusion agenda in a more holistic manner.

In inner-city schools we also need to be concerned about the health and welfare of our staff, who work incredibly hard in such challenging areas. Stress is a factor in such schools. In January 2001 we appointed two trained external partners to offer on a weekly basis a 'reflexology/Indian head massage' drop-in centre for interested staff. I do not believe we can or should underestimate the stress levels of committed and professional colleagues in schools in challenging areas.

A holistic vision of inclusion

At a recent EiC regional conference I overheard a headteacher asking another colleague what he was doing about inclusion in his school. His reply was to state: 'I've got a learning support unit.' I was left thinking, this is not inclusion, in fact, the way it was expressed suggested only in-house exclusion and a short-term strategy for managing difficult students.

There is an African proverb: 'It takes a whole village to educate a child.' I believe that this can be translated in urban areas to: 'It takes a whole city to educate a child.' As such, despite my support for the government's education agenda and appreciation of financial and other resources, I do not believe that schools can make a difference alone. This is particularly problematic in areas of second or third generation unemployment and lack of hope or identity.

If inner-city schools are to become consistently successful and sustain developments, the regeneration process and planning at the level of city councils must also offer strategic support to these beleaguered and isolated areas. As such the regeneration resources relating to Objective 1, Single Regeneration Budget planning, New Deal, Sure Start and New Opportunities funding need to include the schools in these areas in a more joined-up and holistic manner. Urban city council planning in relation to the use of such resources should take account of the school as a valued community resource and should centre its activities around the schools as the community resource that affects the lives of all personnel, parents or otherwise.

Schools alone cannot make a long-term difference to the quality of life, self-esteem and feeling of being valued for adults and families in deprived urban areas. But with some joined-up thinking, planning and resources, then together I believe we could make a difference.

If the government is serious about the life-long learning agenda, I am convinced that community colleges with external support agencies planning and working together could eventually turn areas of no hope into areas of community activity and mutual support. In so doing, the community college or school would be seen as the centre of such activities and planning. Ideally such centres would have a 'one stop shop' resource on the college site or close by, involving external partners for some part of each week, for example, social services, local police, careers and employment advice, housing, tertiary college input, youth service, health support, outreach university staff and city councillors. These personnel need to be situated for some of their time in the inner city areas and not solely in a large and inaccessible building in the centre of the city, where many of our local adults and community personnel lack the confidence to visit. If the regeneration planning is ever to work, then regeneration personnel need to live, breathe and understand the issues of inner-city areas. Community colleges could certainly nurture and support this agenda.

Firth Park Community College opened as a one site college in September 2000 with this planning in mind. We have had some successes to date in community education and life-long learning with a community learning weekend in October, well supported by local people. We are offering evening workshops in ICT, art and leisure-based courses for local community members. Yet these activities are supported by external funding bids or the goodwill of known partners. We should, as an entitlement, be funded beyond the Aggregate Schools Budget to provide such activities if life-long learning is ever to be truly embedded.

Schools should be seen to be a valued resource used regularly by the community for a range of activities, 8 am to 10 pm daily and at weekends. Education should be seen to be a seamless activity in relation to these communities, involving young and old. Such activities may include accredited courses for GCSEs, NVQs, GNVQs, A-levels, Alternative Supplementary (AS) levels and also community meetings, community library resources, leisure activities, drop-in workshops, focus groups – the list goes on. Schools should not be open for just 15 per cent of the year but for the majority of the time and be seen by the community to be a valued, accessible and friendly local provision where community members can meet, learn and support one another.

My vision of Firth Park Community College is to see this ideal becoming a reality. But for this to happen, there needs to be a city-wide view and strategy for community education and inclusion. I want to see our buildings full and bursting at the seams with adults – parents engaging in after-school-hours activities and at weekends in life-long learning in our area of Sheffield. I want to see a pride returning to the Firth Park and Shiregreen communities and an acknowledgement that these people feel they are valued citizens of Sheffield and not just a beleaguered, parochial group who do not belong.

I would like to think that in the next two or three years the college timetable at Firth Park will become less of a college timetable and more of a community timetable, where young people of school age and those engaged in life-long learning will work alongside one another on learning activities. My teaching staff would be able to have flexible contracts, ensuring that they taught the statutory 25 hours, but not necessarily between 8.45 am and 3.15 pm We would deliver the National Curriculum, but would, with other partners, deliver a wider curriculum to the community, both young and old. Community members would wish for an involvement in the college, for their own learning or to offer support, expertise and help in a range of activities, some statutory, others more flexible. With a city-wide view of regeneration and inclusion, all of this is possible, and this could really make a difference.

City council strategies related to regeneration should cease to compartmentalise their activities. We desperately need a strategic vision of education and life-long learning in urban areas to look holistically at the socio-economic divides that include some citizens and exclude others. We need a 10–30-year plan in such areas to ensure a more connected provision of resources and support at all levels, beyond education.

In my area of Sheffield we need some pride and self-esteem for Firth Park and Shiregreen. We need to accept that inclusion is more than just a school-based issue and that schools can be successful only if inclusion is owned by all within the given city. In so doing, schools such as Firth Park Community College will meet and exceed their targets and those achieving this success will wish to put more into their local communities to sustain and develop these initiatives. As these areas have nurtured their success, they will feel a sense of pride and ownership in their local area.

Inclusivity is the responsibility of all who live in urban areas, it is not to do with patronage and funding bids but an issue of city-wide ownership and appropriate resources. Schools on their own can make only a limited difference to the future of young people. But with holistic planning, resources and sustained developments, we could see previously impoverished areas climbing out of the mire of no hope, unemployment and isolation towards a feeling of being included and valued in all that the city aspires to become. This is my hope for Firth Park Community College and its local area.

Reference

DfEE (1999) *Excellence in Cities*, prospectus, March.

12

■ ■ ■

Conclusion

by Irene Dalton, Richard Fawcett and John West-Burnham

In this final chapter we draw together some of the issues that have emerged from the 11 case studies in this book. This is not an attempt to synthesise any generic conclusions but to highlight trends and what we believe to be some of the significant insights available in these accounts of emerging practice. Each account in this collection has integrity in its own right and it would be inappropriate to try to impose a post-hoc rationalisation on case studies that we have invited because of their diversity. However, even the most superficial reading indicates a range of common concerns, initiatives and strategies which are, perhaps, indicative of a profound shift in the conceptualisation of the nature and purpose of education in schools.

Two generic issues need to be addressed before exploring the specific outcomes of these accounts – the notions that are encapsulated in the title of this book, *Schools for the 21st Century,* and the concept of best practice. We will look at these issues first and then consider specific topics: the nature of innovation, the focus on young people, leadership, schools and the community, and the nature of learning.

Schools for the 21st century

Most aspects of human life were subject to speculative musings during the 1990s as to how the move into a new millennium would change them. The reality, of course, was that 1 January 2000 heralded another year in an unbroken progression. There was no sudden tectonic shift in any aspect of society, let alone education. And yet there remains a feeling that the move into the 21st century does provide a significant psychological, if not actual, watershed. It may also be that, irrespective of the chronological dating, there is a sustained movement rather like the early stages of a tsunami, which is calling into question historical patterns of educational provision and beginning to develop a response to a rapidly changing and increasingly turbulent social environment.

Although every school in this collection is reporting radical and innovative practice, they remain schools, recognisable in every respect to preceding generations. This might be entirely proper, valid and inevitable. There is no doubt that over the past decade schools have become far more efficient and effective, and in terms of public accountability measures enormous improvements have taken place. Yet the preoccupation of the writers in this collection is not primarily with government-initiated improvement; it is often with a passionate concern with the educational experiences of young people and their communities. A major question is the extent to which this changing set of priorities can be contained within the historic patterns of schooling.

It has become a banality to argue that schools are essentially 19th-century constructions, yet the fact remains that in many important respects they are. This is not of itself condemnatory, but it does invite significant questioning as to (a) why this is the case and (b) should it be the case? One of our intentions in commissioning these case studies was to contribute to this debate. It is obvious that the students whose experiences are described in these accounts have a rich and varied educational experience provided by caring, dedicated and thoughtful professionals – but at what cost?

The tension between running an essentially archaic schooling system and educating young people to live in the 21st century may well explain the increasing evidence of dysfunction in the school system – problems with recruitment, retention and the well-being of teachers. This tension is likely to increase rather than diminish if even the most cautious view is taken of the potential impact of a range of changes:

- the sustained and unrelenting movement towards performance-based accountability based on reductionist quantitative measures;
- the growing impact of information and communications technology (ICT) on education, which raises profound questions about the 'architecture' of learning – the historic constraints of time and place are being challenged by the explosion in information and new techniques to manage that information;
- the growing awareness of the potential of brain-based learning and developments in cognitive psychology which call into question historic models of psychology;
- the continuing issue of social and economic deprivation and its impact on social expectations and aspirations;
- the fact that Britain remains a society in which racism and sexism are still widespread and social opportunity is still class-related;
- the growing moral ambiguity in society and the lack of any clear ethical consensus;

- the increasing impact of globalisation on the nature of work and leisure;
- the crisis in many communities expressed in crime levels, lack of cohesion and deeply rooted social alienation;
- the fact that ecological issues, the actual survival of the planet, are increasingly important factors in our view of the future.

This list can be redressed by reference to rising academic standards, increased opportunities and a relatively high standard of living. However, no education system can be content if it is successful for some but patently fails others. The articles in this book demonstrate a wide range of responses to many of these issues but within the constraints of an education system originally designed to perpetuate social division and founded on a definition of success that is limited and constrained. There are numerous examples in this book of alternative models of success emerging and schools realigning priorities to meet the real and immediate needs of their students. However, this is within the constraints of reductionist measures of outcomes, limited access to education (as opposed to schooling) and a system where organisational imperatives assume a higher status than individual needs.

Schools *in* the 21st century face an immensely complex task in bridging the movement from an antiquated model of schooling to the development of schools *for* the 21st century. The shape of schools in the future is impossible to predict, but the issues that feature in these studies provide a powerful indication of the shape of education to come.

Best practice

The concept of best practice is complex and has many worrying undercurrents. The tension is essentially between a desire to recognise and celebrate what is manifestly an example of appropriate and effective practice, and an anxiety about any attempts to preach one best way or to advocate conformity. Much educational reform of recent years has been posited on the basis of the replication of authoritatively defined best practice. The literacy and numeracy strategies are classic examples of this. The Office for Standards in Education (Ofsted) framework represents the most sustained and comprehensive modelling of best practice in any education system in democratic societies.

In presenting the case studies in this book we are not presuming to propose models of practice to be replicated. What we are offering are examples of processes that lead to a range of outcomes that are right in a given context at a given time. The problem with any definition of best practice is that it codifies one perspective and inevitably this can lead to ossification and the reification of one viewpoint. On the other hand, there is an issue of equity in this: if successful strategies can be identified and if they are proven to work, should they not be available to all?

What is clear is that any attempt to define best practice and then promulgate it can lead to the lowest common denominator becoming policy and thereby constraining and inhibiting innovation. Fundamental to any definition is the value system that the best practice is derived from and so serves as the basis of prioritisation. Recent years in the English education system have seen an appropriate focus on what might be described as basic skills. The emphasis on this area has naturally served as a focus for resources, energy and priorities to the exclusion, if not the detriment, of other aspects of education.

However worthy the priorities implicit to recent national policies, questions have to be raised as to the sustainability of centrally imposed definitions and the extent to which centrally prescribed strategies diminish capability and capacity at school level. We regard the case studies in this collection as evidence of best practice derived from:

- creativity at school level;
- concerns for process and outcomes;
- response to real needs;
- inherent sustainability and capacity building.

As we have already argued, the shape of education in the future is impossible to predict and so, therefore, is best practice in the future. We offer these examples of best practice to stimulate debate and creativity, not to impose conformity or to suggest that there is one answer to the issues that face schools.

Innovation

One of the distinguishing features of the schools in this collection is their commitment to innovation. For many years, the management of change has been seen as a central component of effective education management. The language of this aspect of school life has tended to focus on change as an event, as a specific issue to be dealt with before resuming the normal patterns of management. Change was perceived as an interruption to the norm.

Central to the accounts in this book is an awareness of change as a process – a permanent characteristic of organisational life – and that a key feature of the school of the future is the capacity to innovate, to create a culture in which changing is the norm, to create strategies to improve and to translate the vision and moral aspirations of the school into actual practice. If it is true that the rapidly changing environment in which schools increasingly have to operate is now the norm, then the responses to that environment have to be commensurately radical. Fundamental changes in the demands on schools require fundamentally different responses – we do not improve by doing more of what we have always done.

Educational policy making remains profoundly conservative – improving the efficiency of the journey, without ever questioning the destination. National policy making can never serve as the impetus for profound improvement because it has to satisfy too many contradictory stakeholders. One policy can never fit all needs; it is easy to prescribe solutions, but profound change can occur only at institutional level.

Such profound change is rooted in innovations, as is demonstrated in the case studies. Innovation involves a fundamental and systematic reappraisal of why something is done and how it is best done. Innovation is a classical example of lateral thinking – challenging norms, comfortable patterns of operating, and shifting the *a priori* on which planning takes place. The numerous examples of innovation in this book point to a number of fundamental characteristics:

- courage – the willingness to be different, to be comfortable with the loss of the status quo and to sustain the process against the odds;
- creativity – in spite of all the daily demands and routines, the schools in this book show a remarkable talent to generate original responses to historic problems;
- consistency – innovation is a continuous process, a way of life, the culture of the school, affecting everyone and every aspect of the school's life;
- challenge – the creation of a culture of questioning, of analysis and review, an intellectual restlessness; in other words, a culture of shared enquiry and real learning.

National policies do not enhance capability, nor do they contribute to sustainability – they tend to drain and diminish. Sustainable improvement has to be rooted in schools responding to real needs and able to develop capability. National reforms come and go, but the long-term development of education resides in the creativity of schools.

Focus on young people

No one can doubt the fundamental and profound commitment to the welfare and care of young people shown by the education profession. It is therefore strange, if not actually bizarre, that the British education system lacks a formalised statement about the rights of those who are being educated. This is not about legal provision but rather the moral basis of schooling. A useful starting point might be to consider the notion of a young person's entitlement. The right to education is enshrined in law and is a fundamental component of any model of human rights. However, this guarantees only the existence of education – it says very little about the content of that education and in particular the experience of education.

Access to education is guaranteed in law and implemented through policy. The experience of education grows out of provision at local level, the nature of human relationships and the quality and richness of the opportunities available. One of the outstanding features of these case studies is the focus on the actual experience of children and young people. On the basis of these accounts it is possible to advance a number of propositions about the moral basis of young people's experience in schools:

- well-being is central to successful education: all members of the school community need to experience physical, emotional, psychological and social well-being – it is impossible to learn, grow and develop as a person unless there is a fundamental guarantee of well-being;

- a sense of personal value, of self-worth with positive self-esteem, is prerequisite to any debate about the nature and content of the educational process;

- opportunities for success in personally significant terms must be fundamental to the design and implementations of all educational experiences;

- there must be a sense of joy, wonder and fun for every individual as the most significant component of the experience of school.

This list is not intended to be exclusive, exhaustive or prescriptive, but these elements are to be found, implicitly or explicitly, in every account in this book. One of the fundamental issues for schools in the 21st century must be the development of a consensual ethical base for education that informs the daily lives of all children. The moral experience of education has to become the primary focus for accountability.

Leadership

So much has been written about leadership in education in recent years that it is difficult to see what can usefully be added to the oppressive weight of rhetoric burdening education professionals. Yet these studies often reveal, sometimes unwittingly, aspects of leadership that are not amenable to neat categorisation.

The first and most significant point is that all the schools in this collection are led, and not just managed. The distinction between leadership and management is more than just semantic. The past ten years have seen enormous pressures on schools to improve the quality of management. By and large this has happened, and British schools are among the best managed in the world. However, the response to the demands to manage more and more efficiently have in some instances 'driven out' leadership. There is only so much time and energy available and the combination of site management and policy implementation has been a profound drain. What is remarkable in this context is that the quality of leadership in many schools has actually grown. The case studies reveal three critical components of leadership as distinct from management:

- firstly, there is a profound concern with how things should be, a clear sense of the future and the ability to articulate the components of a robust and relevant vision;
- secondly, there is a clear sense of values as the means by which the vision should be attained – the accounts in this book all reveal a strong sense of moral purpose and shared priorities;
- thirdly, there is a strong sense of the importance of personal relationships – the essential basis for any successful community.

Another central theme is the collaborative basis of planning and implementation. This is more than the usual rhetoric surrounding teams, as it involves a genuine sense of community involvement and engagement. Inclusivity in decision making in one of the most difficult aspects of school life to achieve – it requires a wide range of leadership qualities. The creativity and innovation shown in the case studies can never be the result of one individual's efforts, however gifted they might be. However, this is not to diminish the importance of leadership provided by the headteacher and the leadership team. The drive, energy and development of capacity and capability needed to implement major innovations have to be balanced by the need for accountability, the deployment of resources, the development of individuals and the creation of a supportive infrastructure.

Leadership, as demonstrated in these case studies, is a central and crucial variable in the creation of schools for the 21st century. While strong and purposeful individual leadership is vital, it has to be matched by the development of leadership in depth. Leadership is not the status of the few but the activity of the many.

Schools and the community

There are many historical factors that conspire to isolate schools from their communities, the most significant of which is the exclusivity of schools as organisations – pupils, teachers and support staff only. In this sense, schools have been 'closed' organisations with limited and controlled access, single usage and very limited utilisation in terms of time. Many schools have been *in* their communities but not *of* their communities.

One of the most significant changes manifested in the development of schools for the 21st century is a reconceptualisation of the relationship between schools and their environments. Several of the case studies demonstrate what might be termed community integration, with the school becoming a resource for the community on equal terms with its statutory educational function. There is a clear awareness that one of the key factors in raising achievement is raising the status of education in the community – this means enhancing the significance of the school and making it an inclusive organisation.

A community *qua* community has a number of fundamental characteristics:

- there is a shared values system;
- the community is inclusive;
- the community is a safe place;
- there is parity of access to resources;
- social and economic issues are addressed collaboratively.

The concept of community education has a long and distinguished history but it has always been partial, often operating on a grace and favour basis. Too often the school was synonymous with its buildings rather than being one of the users of a shared resource. If education is to be a shared community activity, then schooling and school can no longer be synonymous. What the case studies demonstrate is more than physical access; they show a deliberate attempt to increase a sense of shared ownership through shared usage on the basis of parity of esteem.

A further important implication of full community integration is that pupils have increased opportunities to become involved in their communities and to learn the implications of participation as citizens in democratic societies. Community responsibility cannot be taught – it has to be learned through real-life experiences that are significant and authentic.

The nature of learning

By way of conclusion to this summary, it is worth reflecting on the most significant unifying factor in these case studies. All of them, directly and indirectly, are concerned with the nature of learning for pupils. One of the most significant current educational trends is the increasing understanding of the nature of learning. This development builds on the historic development of the nature of teaching and the centrality of the curriculum. What is sometimes referred to as the 'science of learning' has emerged in recent years to increase our confidence in understanding the nature of learning as a process.

There are three components to this increased understanding:

- the advances in neurological science, which have enhanced our understanding of how brain functioning and learning are inextricably linked;
- developments in cognitive psychology, which have enhanced our ability to understand the processes that are most likely to enhance learning for understanding;
- an enhanced awareness of the impact of social relationships on learning.

The overall impact of these trends has been to force a significant re-evaluation of the nature of pedagogy, learning as an individual process, and the role of the teacher. This in turn has profound implications for the conceptualisation of the school as a place appropriate to facilitate the learning process.

While all the case studies show a fundamental concern about learning, some demonstrate the dramatic impact of the new understanding. This inevitably forces profound analysis of the historic patterns of working and the consideration of a range of new strategies and techniques. It would be naïve to underestimate the difficulty in bringing about changes to the core purpose of every school. But this allows us to draw the single most important conclusion from these case studies.

In developing schools for the 21st century the dominant factor is the willingness of educational professionals to reconceptualise the nature of the work they do. Every case study is characterised by a readiness to engage with new ideas, to review, analyse and question historic practice in a profound and fundamental way. There are numerous trends impinging on schools – some may be short term, others profound in their potential implications. There can be no one set model for schools of the future, no one right answer. The diversity represented in these studies is one of the most significant features of the response to a changing world. What is common is the willingness to engage in a process of profound questioning and develop new solutions to the fundamental issues affecting schools. At the heart of every case study is the professional integrity, commitment to young people and desire to improve that characterise educational leadership in our schools.

Index

■ ■ ■